Report Verses in
Rudolf Steiner's
Art of Education

Report Verses in Rudolf Steiner's Art of Education

Healing Forces in Words and Their Rhythms

Heinz Muller

Floris Books

Translated by Jesse Darrell

First published in German in 1967 under the title
Von der heilenden Kraft des Wortes und der Rhythmen
by Verlag Freies Geistesleben, Stuttgart
First published in English in 1983
by Steiner Waldorf Schools Fellowship Publications
as *Healing Forces in the Word and its Rhythms*

Copyright © 1967 Verlag Freies Geistesleben, Stuttgart
English version © 1983, 2013 Steiner Waldorf Schools Fellowship Publications

Second edition published in 2013 by Floris Books in
association with the Steiner Waldorf Schools Fellowship

British Library CIP Data available
ISBN 978-086315-988-6

Printed in Great Britain
by Page Bros Ltd.

Contents

Translator's note on pronounciation

The vowel sounds in the text follow German pronounciation. Equivalent English approximations are as follows:

A – as in "ah" (art)
E – as in "eh" (ate)
I – as in "ee" (eat)
O – as in "oh" (oat)
U – as in "oo" (boot)
Au – as in "ow" (out)
Ei – as in personal pronoun "I" (bite)

Ch – as in Scots "loch", *not* as in "cheese"

Translator's Foreword

The education of children today needs above all to work therapeutically, a principle which was at the heart of every aspect of the Waldorf pedagogy Rudolf Steiner instituted after the First World War. Steiner drew attention to the living realities in speech and language, and to the artistic and therefore healing role they should be enabled to play in modern education. One recommendation he made – coming immediately to the theme of this book – was for teachers to write verses for their children, to be inserted in their annual school reports which, through their form and content, would help the child's development. In this book Heinz Müller explains the guiding principles which Steiner advised him to follow in such a work and, while indicating the particular difficulties he was trying to help his children overcome, offers a considerable selection of the verses he himself composed during his many years as a Waldorf class teacher. These verses, it should be noted, were repeated by the children at weekly intervals throughout the year. I have not, by any means, translated all of these, but enough to illustrate the principles of composition he uses in relation to the various needs of his pupils. I can only hope that the English form I have given them will convey something of what he achieved for the children, and that these concrete examples of Steiner's foundational advice will stimulate readers into a similar therapeutic activity of their own.

The inspiration that can be found in Heinz Müller's little book, by everyone who is searching for an approach to teaching which is adequate for our increasingly chaotic times, derives not least from the impression it conveys of the author himself as a wise, loving and endlessly conscientious man and teacher.

Jesse Darrell

Note to the second edition

Written almost fifty years ago, this book still offers helpful stimulus and suggestions for modern-day Waldorf teachers. The language of the verses is obviously not that of today, but their background, rhythm, alliteration and remarks can nonetheless inspire teachers to work fruitfully on their own verses.

Introduction

After being a teacher for forty-two years in the Rudolf Steiner School at Wandsbek in Hamburg, where I had been sent in 1923 by Rudolf Steiner himself, I have used the leisure granted me in my latter years to recall and think over what I had done in the calling so dear to me. In seeking the inner sources of that joyful activity, I found that from earliest childhood, it was as if lines of guidance had rayed through my life, and the themes of my life's endeavour had made themselves heard, again and yet again. Indeed I came to see that the prelude was an integral part of the whole composition, and that later variations could be understood only if the earlier intimations of the basic themes were not passed over.

My first love was for the Word. As far back as I can remember, my early days had been accompanied by the solemn utterance of prayers and verses from the Bible. I felt them to be as much a necessity of life as daily bread itself. Most beautiful of all for me, however, were the fairy tales which, to my mind, no one could tell as well as my grandmother. While still just a child, I could already relate a fair number of them, thanks to my good memory and powers of imitation, and which made my playmates happy. Another thing was that we had our meeting places among the monastery ruins at

Paulinzella, and there we never tired of listening to the mysterious echoes among their niches and arches of what we sang or called out.

Yet another experience came when visiting parties of students and young theologians struck up with their songs and hymns in Latin or Greek among the ruins; we fairly trembled with awe as we listened to these unfamiliar sounds. We didn't understand them at all, but let ourselves be borne aloft by just the music and rhythm of the singing. It was this, after all, which enlivened our own counting verses when we had recourse to them in our games. Quite innocent of meaning, one of them ran as follows:

> Ehne dehne dicke nelle,
> Wische wasche bombe schelle,
> Bombe schie, bombe schah,
> Wische wasche dowirah.

I came to know other forms of spoken sound that were full of mystery for me from people connected with our family who practised herb-gathering along old traditional lines. At certain times of the year, at sunrise and sunset, when herbs were being picked and prepared for all kinds of home-made remedies, ancient verses and blessings were always impressively repeated. The fine-smelling essences were sent far afield with remarkable names like Pain-Expeller or Hingfong Tincture. When using some of these, certain healing benedictions had to be said to enhance their effectiveness. How often did our grandmother utter such a form of words, repeated several times over, when we had hurt ourselves! We had no doubt that it would help. It was a matter of course that the preparation of many foods, especially the baking of bread, was accompanied with appropriate sayings. Moreover we children could hear words spoken with special earnestness when the adults, withdrawn for the occasion into another room, were in deep devotion engaged with their inner preparation for Holy Communion next morning.

When I was about ten years old I had to take the entrance exam for the classical grammar school. As I was exempt from the oral test in arithmetic, I was taken into a senior class while the others were going through this, and here I experienced the first history lesson of my life. What was told there seemed somehow familiar to me out of a long-distant past. Pictures arose in me which my imagination worked on in the liveliest fashion. What I heard did not always correspond with what I was inwardly experiencing. I have often since wondered about strange things like this: I had certainly never heard anything before about the conflagration in Ephesus or the birth of Alexander the Great on that disastrous night, and yet I seemed to be closely familiar with many scenes concerned with it. Moreover there came from the teacher's lips words which were full of secret meaning to me, such as "mystery-wisdom" and "self-knowledge", and Greek words also whose tones had once been heard in Diana's temple, and were to resound again at the beginning of the Gospel of John.

My first history lesson was so full of questions and mysteries for me that everything else I experienced at that time paled beside it. Turning to the first verses of John's Gospel, I was naturally none the wiser for my first reading of them, and indeed even more perplexed and unsettled. When an older pupil said these same words in Greek, the sounds I heard again made a very deep impression on me, but of course answered none of the questions I found so puzzling. I tried to put them aside, but every attempt at this was quite unsuccessful. I then went as far as reading something about Alexander the Great, about his earlier years in particular but also about his later heroic deeds, and was filled to overflowing with enthusiasm.

Eleven years later, the first words of John's Gospel again met me in a special moment of destiny. On the previous day I had received permission as a teaching student to visit classes for the first time in the Waldorf School in Stuttgart. I went along quite early to the Kanonenweg [since renamed Hausmannstrasse] and walked up and down in front of the school, watching the teachers and children as they streamed towards it from all directions. And then, ascending the last of some nearby steps with heavy tread, there came into view a man with a big head and with strongly marked features like a peasant. He stopped in astonishment when, without hesitation, I greeted him. He looked inquiringly at me and then said, "We don't know each other, do we?"

When I said we did not, he continued, "Now, isn't that a real pleasure? A lovely morning like this with sunshine, and birds all chirping away, and here's a young man I don't know in front of me, and greets me like a friend."

He said other things too, all with an intonation unmistakably Austrian, and then came an unexpected turn. "My name's Karl; what is yours?"

"Heinz," I said.

"Heinz, we are good friends. Come along with me; I have to go over to the Waldorf School to my children."

Thus it was that I entered the grounds of the school at the side of Dr Karl Schubert. While he went into a wooden building to his class, I went to the school office and there asked Rudolf Steiner which class I should visit. He told me how to get to a certain classroom where I was to knock and say I had been sent by him to sit in. I knocked and almost the next moment Schubert opened the door.

"I thought you'd be coming to me today," he said, and at once introduced me to his class. In it there were all ages of children, some to get special help just for a few weeks or months and then go back to their own classes, others needing help as a special group all the time. Schubert stood behind me with his hands on my shoulders and peeping out – I was quite a lot taller than he – first on one side and then on the other. Then he said, "Dear children, it's a great pleasure I have today, as a good friend has come to visit us. And as I like him so much, you must like him as well."

I then made as if to go and sit unobtrusively at the back, but Schubert would not have that at all and instead gave me something special to do. He called out a big awkward lad who he said must be got to the point of speaking, without delay. He had himself been repeating the first words of St John's Gospel with

15

him every day, and I was now to take this over. With each word in Greek, which had to be spoken out loud, the boy had to stamp one step forward. So after the morning verse and some exercises that all the children did, I took charge of the boy and set about the speaking and stamping. Meanwhile, it had become very hot in the room, with the sun now shining strongly through the windows and sending its heat through the flat roof of the wooden building, which was covered with black roofing felt. Karl Schubert himself went on teaching the rest of the class while we carried on behind him with stamping and declaiming our *"en arche"*. Suddenly he turned round and asked why I was saying it so quietly. Couldn't I do it louder?

I said I would then disturb his own teaching; he dismissed this, however, and in a booming voice demonstrated how he wanted it done. That was the start, for us, of a strenuous sweat-cure, for the longer it continued, the more energetically I had to urge on the ever-inert colossus beside me to do his stamping. Finally, after something like fifty minutes of this, the two of us came to an exhausted halt for a breather at the open window. In something between a sigh and a groan, but unmistakably approximating to the words we'd just been practising, the panting youth said, *"En arche en ho logos."*

For each word he used a deep, full breath. Karl Schubert at once turned round and listened with the utmost intentness. Then he clapped first the boy and then myself on the shoulder, and jubilantly announced, "I knew this straight off this morning: it's a glorious day; the sun is shining, the birds singing, a young friend greets me – and you, my boy, speak the first words of your life."

The next term in my teacher training began, and during my course in Jena I had to face a first important test by taking a fourth class of children. After no more than a few days the timetable had to be altered on my account, for I had to have a free period after every two lessons to give my flagging voice a chance to recover. After two further lessons, however, I was usually as hoarse as a crow. I tried every possible means and method of speech therapy during the following months, but all in vain; my voice went from bad to worse. This became the more depressing the more I enjoyed the actual teaching and – apart from my voice problem – the more this promised well for the future.

Coming once more to visit classes in the Waldorf School at Easter 1922, I had scarcely entered the school grounds when I met Rudolf Steiner. He took me to his room and on the way asked me how it had gone with my first experience of teaching.

"I'm beginning to think," I replied, "that I won't be able to go on with it, as I have such difficulties with my voice."

When we got to his room Rudolf Steiner at once came back to this and so, as I had in fact already decided to do before setting out, I ventured to put the following question: "You gave the teachers of the Waldorf School a great number of speech exercises during the courses before the opening of the school. Could you also advise how to correct one's own mistakes and deficiencies in speaking, and how to work with speech in a healing and educational way?"

Rudolf Steiner suggested we began with the first part of my query, and asked me what I thought myself should be done if speech defects were to be put right. Up to that moment I had always been utterly at a loss in the matter, but now I was able to say something in reply; it was as if in Rudolf Steiner's presence, many things now came to one, but above all as if his kind of listening and questioning opened a way to answers one wouldn't have reached so easily on one's own. So I stammered out something of what I thought would have to be done if any healing through speech was to be achieved. To my utter astonishment Rudolf Steiner said this was very good and encouraged me to go on. For a moment once again I was at a loss, and then once again a couple of ideas came to me which he entirely agreed with. This happened twice more, after which not even with concentrated reflection could I think of anything further. Thereupon Rudolf Steiner said he would like to give special consideration to this question in the summer, and invited me to come as guest to Haus Hansi, where he lived, for the six weeks beginning at the end of July, and take part in the work.

Nearly everything which Rudolf Steiner then worked out in a small circle for the first time during this period appeared two years later in the Drama Course, and can be studied in detail there *(Speech and Drama)*. The second part of my question *was* dealt with in many conversations in the course of these two years; for the most part they consisted of brief suggestions and observations which Rudolf Steiner made whenever I told him of the difficulties of particular pupils of mine.

One of the first things he said was, "Cultivate speech in yourself and your children with the greatest care, since far and away the most of what a teacher gives his children comes to them on the wings of speech." When talking to children, one should never out of mere carelessness use a banal expression. Of course that doesn't mean one should go in for high-flown appeals to the feelings. "Banality and hollow sentimentalising shut out real heart and especially real humour straight away. Just these two, however, are a teacher's most important helpers as he shepherds his flock along."

In trying to pass on the suggestions and indications which Rudolf Steiner gave me for the handling and cultivation of speech – the many conversations in which he did so, incidentally, began for the most part on his side, as I myself only occasionally asked to speak with him – I have a difficulty. All my notes about these things went up in the flames of the stupendous firestorms in Hamburg during 1943. Much has vanished from memory, and here and there I have modified some things on account of my practical experience with them; all the same, nothing has been in any way misreported. May this work therefore be received from the very beginning with consideration and goodwill.

What are Report Verses
and How are They Used
in Teaching?

When the Waldorf School was founded in Stuttgart
on September 22, 1919, the question came up of how
often and in what form reports were to be given. At
first Rudolf Steiner thought they should be given twice
a year, but it soon became obvious that neither the
authorities nor the parents were expecting this. So it
became the practice to give reports at the end of each
school year.

On the report forms, a large space is reserved for
what the class teacher has to say about the pupil in
question. Rudolf Steiner attached the greatest value to
making as individual a picture of the child as possible.
In doing this, one was to avoid negative comments.
Teachers were to go deeply into the character, the
abilities but also the deficiencies and weaknesses of
their pupils in as loving a way as they could, and to
present everything with unfailing goodwill. Only after
this should there follow something of an assessment
of what had been accomplished. The picture thus put
forward must, of course, be really faithful and free of

distortion. But there was also to be no suggestion of sitting in judgment or condemnation; rather one was to show how an improvement was to be brought about. Whereas with the younger classes this part of the report was to be directed exclusively to the parents, in the middle school one was also to address the children themselves. Without the slightest appeal to ambition, teachers were to find loving, appreciative words of encouragement even for the dullest of their charges, and in a similar way one could, with humour, make an impression even on the biggest rascal. Finally, class teachers were to sum up in a verse what they considered should accompany the pupil as inner guidance during the following year.

In a College meeting on May 26, 1921 Rudolf Steiner indicated succinctly what he expected in reports. "We are agreed that we should write the reports as we did last year. As faithful a picture as possible; at the end once more a verse that can show the individual child the direction in which it should strive." On various occasions he emphasised it was good for teachers to make the verse up themselves.

What with the advertisements, traffic turmoil and the like that they meet with on their way to school, especially in large cities, children arrive in a condition that needs remedying as far as possible before one can reasonably begin any work. It is, above all, important that the noise and tumult of the streets should not be continued into the classroom. The teacher can best achieve this by seeing that the children wait quietly to be greeted with a handshake, before they enter

21

the classroom. One must then stay with them till the bell goes for lessons to begin. During this time there may be notes for the parents to be given out, perhaps money to be collected, or things to be got ready for a painting lesson, which is usually held each week. At the beginning of the lesson, teacher and children together say a morning verse. Then there comes some music, with younger children playing block pipes or recorders in unison, and later on other instruments as well. As well as this there is practice in choral singing with instrumental accompaniment. Finally a series of speech exercises is done by the children either individually or together, which should strive for the utmost precision. After this, it is time for the report verses to be recited.

If one has only a small number of children, one can perhaps let them all say their verses each day. In the big classes, however, which I myself had, it was a matter of dividing up the children, which led to some interesting groupings. I arranged that every child said their verse on the day of the week on which they were born, with the Sunday-children leading off on Monday mornings. To begin with, in the earlier weeks of the new school year, I myself first said each verse using as good speech as possible, but later on this was no longer necessary. It was often astonishing to see how remarkable karmic correspondences showed themselves in the groups arising out of the weekdays of birth. In one class, for example, there was a Wednesday group in which many of the children needed something special doing for their health, as if they had sought out the Mercury day for their entry on to the earth. Or children who had already been friends before they began to attend school would find themselves in the same verse-group through their birth on the same weekday. I can recommended every class teacher investigates such weekday connections. The experiences gained in this way are for the most part so delicate and intimate that one hesitates to put them into words.

After all these preliminaries, the children are ready for the lesson itself, free now from any outside influences that could disturb or endanger the work. The most important thing of all is that, through an intimately artistic way of working, children are enabled to receive what the teaching offers quite differently from how they can when they are simply approached intellectually. It is one of the greatest joys of a class teacher, when visiting the parents, to discover how just the report verses have come to such life in the children. They will often be heard talking among themselves about their verses with a real pride in them. The teacher can then hope that the word has indeed made its way into the feeling and the will, just as Rudolf Steiner expressed it:

> Far more than with our thinking the word binds
> together with our feeling, and far more strongly again
> with everything that lies in the will. Feeling belongs to a
> much more unconscious part of the soul than thinking,
> and the will to a still less conscious part than feeling. For
> our thinking the words we speak amount to little more,
> as it were, than signs. To our feeling they have a far more
> intimate connection. They join forces with feeling far

more closely, and especially closely do they do so with the will.*

How much responsibility there is, therefore, in the work with report verses, and how great is the healing we can achieve through them if we strive hard with them, with all our might.

* 'The Realm of Language,' July 17, 1915.

Rhythms and their Application

Speech did not originate in the speaking we use in ordinary life any more than writing originated in the writing of today. Compare the latter with the picture-writing of ancient Egypt; that will give you some idea of how writing first came about. And it is just as useless to look for the origin of speech in the ordinary talking of today which contains all manner of acquired qualities – conventional, intellectual, and so on. No, speech has its source in the artistic life. And if we want, in our study of speech, to find our way through to what is truly artistic, we must at least have begun to perceive that speech originates in the artistic side of man's nature – not in the intellectual, not in the human life of knowledge, as knowledge is understood today. Time was when people were incapable of speaking without rhythm, when they felt a need whenever they spoke to always speak in rhythm.*

I first came to ask about using speech as a healing aid for a particular child when Rudolf Steiner was informing himself about every one of the children in my first class – a small one – in the Waldorf School

* *Speech and Drama,* page 28.

in Wandsbek in Hamburg. He had sent me there, as I mentioned, at Easter 1923. After our first talk about my class he not only knew every child by name, but also all their characteristics as I had described them, and as were indicated also in the paintings and drawings I had shown him. He had a clear picture of them even down to their social and family circumstances. And afterwards he inquired about every single child whenever he saw me at a conference or during the holidays in Stuttgart.

There was a girl in my class who was always in danger of losing herself; she was very sanguine and nervous and her speech was more like that of a younger child. It was much too high, a kind of cheeping, with the *I* (English *ee)* and *E* (as in late) sounds in particular often shrill and irritating. Rudolf Steiner's advice here was to write a verse for the child with short lines, each one of which passed from a strongly emphasised word at the beginning to one similarly emphatic at the end. For just this child, it was important for the teacher to take the trouble to compose such a verse himself. "That's possible for every teacher," he smilingly added. He dispensed with the objection that with a poor verse one might even harm the child, by saying, "You would be letting the child repeat the verse from time to time. If it were really bad, you would very soon feel so unhappy about it you would waste no time in trying to make something better."

The rhythm resulting from this first indication, the *choriamb* (– ˘ ˘ –) in which two unaccented syllables stand between two accented, has something awakening, arresting about it, especially through the emphasis at the end of a line being followed immediately by that at the beginning of the next. In each line a quality of clear, purposeful striving prevails. It is important with this kind of verse that every line should be spoken on a full single breath.

A verse which took shape on the basis of the above indication went as follows:

1.
> Wake, thou my head,
> Love, thou my heart,
> Help, thou my hand!
> What then I do,
> Right will it be,
> Fair, rev'rent, good.

In the last line there are three emphasised syllables and only one unemphasised. A deliberate change of rhythm always has an arousing effect. In the actual saying of the verse, one must take care that the change of rhythm comes out clearly.

Later on I also used the same rhythm frequently for choleric children, especially with those liable to get really wild. Occasionally the metre was changed in the last line into three *trochees* (– ˘), in the last of which the short syllable was left out. A more tranquil element comes into verses given this turn, which awakens reflection and ultimately deliberation and self-awareness.

2.   Head that folly thinks,
                Weak in work 'twill be:
                Hand that hits and shoves
                Takes hold clumsily.
                God gave me my head
                To learn with; gave me too
                Hands both left and right,
                Skilful work to do.

A verse for a sanguine child:

3. As the clamorous stream down the hillside comes leaping,
     O'er reef and o'er rock in high sport,
     With a foaming and frothing its course gaily keeping,
     In joy it sets distance at naught.

     Now flows it to the mill the vale along,
     And turns the mill wheel great;
     Works on and on, calm, careful, strong,
     From early until late.

Rudolf Steiner spoke also of other things which need to be taken into account when making report verses. For example, in choosing the metre to be used it is a good thing to start off with one that goes along with the temperament of the child. Thus with sanguine children you should begin with light, dancing syllables and then come to rest by way of emphasised syllables. In the first lines you could use the *anapest* (˘ ˘ –) and then change to the *iamb* (˘ –). For phlegmatic children the opposite would hold

good: you could lead them over from the *trochee* (– ˘)
to the *dactyl* (– ˘ ˘).

As an aside, Steiner made a comparison with
Hahnemann's homoeopathic method of healing like
with like. With a sanguine child, for example, the
picture in the verse should be of something passing
from movement to rest; whereas with a phlegmatic
child, it would need to go the opposite way.

A verse for a phlegmatic child:

4.
> Water 'neath the hill top lies.
> Still, deep hid from view,
> Till at last from sleep 'twould rise,
> Valiant deeds to do.
>
> Down it streams through clefts confining,
> Distant woodland scents divining,
> Till at last from dark escaping,
> Into sunlight it comes leaping.
>
> Jubilant greeting the wood birds now sing,
> Glad at the life-gift that flows from the spring.

In the last two lines, small changes in rhythm have
again been purposely made; besides their moving into
dactyls, we have the verse-foot "wood birds now"
with two emphasised syllables at the beginning rather
than two unemphasised at the end. We have the same
thing again in the last line with the second foot. A
more intimate feeling for these rhythmic variations
makes plain that they can be consciously followed only

with a noticeably increased effort of will, which is just what is called for with phlegmatic children. However questionable such liberties may be artistically, there is everything to be said for them pedagogically.

Rudolf Steiner once pointed out how unnecessary it was for teachers to intersperse their stories and verses with moral admonitions. Where the picture or story employed is sufficiently clear and penetrating, the individuality of the child extracts from it what they need. Before the age of twelve, children can seldom bring to clear consciousness how a verse or a story relates to themselves. On the other hand, I have often had the experience of saying a new verse in front of the class for the first time and the children at once recognising whom among them it was meant for.

Just how strongly young adults can continue to feel their connection with a verse they received at school when they were children was once brought home to me by a former pupil. After taking her exams she sent me the report verse she had been given in her eleventh year, and wrote that this had been a guidance to her in every circumstance up till then. It went as follows:

5. In nooks and crannies 'neath woodland's deep shade
   There ferns and soft mosses are growing;
   No colours have they to light up the dim glade,
   As have roses in gardens a-glowing.
   Yet small though they may be,
   They're fashioned most finely.
   Great wonders of God we discern
   E'en in algae and moss and in fern.

Now a young woman, she said that this verse had said a great deal to her in regard to her childhood vanity, and had been a real help in her struggle with it. Exactly this had been intended when the verse was written fourteen years earlier, although nothing had ever passed between us previously about this particular weakness. Another former student, who had long since become a mother with a whole flock of children, sent me her report verse from the second year of school and said that it had helped time and again to arouse her sense of responsibility in face of life's demands.

6. God this to the choir of the angels told:
"All beings shall follow your will.
Continue creation in forms manifold,
That my heart with joy you may fill."
Then spoke they to man with loving speech:
"In the likeness divine hadst thou birth.
Create thou also, and its goal thus reach
For this heavenly star, for this Earth."

It is the *amphibrach*, the "short on either side" (⏑ – ⏑), which gives the metrical foundation here. This rhythm is particularly good for melancholic children.

Choleric children, on the other hand, have a liking for lines beginning with a *spondee* (– –):

7. Huge powers upsurge,
Storm, rage in fear,
All things draw near
Dark ruin's verge.

> But giant powers that can destroy,
> When used with love such service yield,
> That they become to man's great joy
> The noble spirit's sword and shield.

In accordance with a suggestion of Rudolf Steiner's, it has been found that for children who stammer or even stutter, hexameters made up of the distinctest possible dactyls (– ᵕ ᵕ) can be specially helpful. Here every effort should be made to avoid the stress coinciding with the consonant or vowel which usually trips or holds up the child. In particularly difficult cases, where the child struggles with every plosive or initial impact consonant such as *D* and *K* (*Stosslaut*) and every possible vowel, one is often left with only aspirants or blown sounds such as *V* and *F* (*Blaselaut*). A repetition of initial consonants such as is found in the alliteration of all earlier northern European poetry is, of course, entirely out of place, artistically speaking, in Greek-style hexameters, but for badly afflicted stutterers such an artistic anomaly has proved a powerful aid.

A verse of this kind which helped a stutterer in the fourth year went thus:

8.
> Odin, the wisest of wanderers,
> Works in the wind and the weather:
> Warmth through man's word he sends wafting,
> Awak'ning the wonder of wisdom.

Breathing as a Factor
in Healing

We arrive now at the treatment of those difficulties which arise out of irregularities in breathing. Asthmatics, for instance, are not suffering in the first place from a shortage of breath: it is much more a matter of not being able to rid themselves of the used-up breath in their lungs. This can be seen from the excessive arching of the patient's chest. Now it has no sense, of course, to admonish an asthmatic during a bad attack to make a full expulsion of their breath; in such a condition, only a doctor can help. But perhaps the speech instructor can do something to avert the worst of the trouble by working against the tendency of not letting the air stream come out freely when speaking. The colds and the chills which children so often have to put up with nowadays – not to mention adults and even teachers – can best be counteracted by encouraging patients not to breathe in again with even a trace of air inside them. Consistent practice in this direction can even stave off a cold. On one occasion, Rudolf Steiner made the patient spit vigorously at the end of each line! There was something particularly comic about this as the spitting was performed at the end of such stately lines as:

> In the vast, the measureless world-wide spaces ...
> In the rounds of time unending ...

Finally the speaker could contain himself no longer and burst out laughing, upon which Rudolf Steiner smiled and said, "Laughing is such a healthy thing, you see, simply because you can't keep back any breath. You don't interrupt a hearty laugh to get a new breath until you have used up every bit of the old air inside you."

When their period of prohibition came to an end in 1946 and the Waldorf Schools could begin again, I took on a class of children of whom some were over ten years of age. At first the class seemed generally unable "to come into the breath". Before any speech exercise, I had to make sure that the whole class got a little out of breath, through some sort of energetic movement.

Another threat to good speaking came through droning and letting the end of each line sink down. These two things make it impossible to be really awake in what one is saying. Even in classes which have done their speech exercises and poems from the first year of school on with a clear guidance of the breath-stream, the danger of mere droning or sing-song comes in again with the end of the second and throughout the third class. For the most part it is the monotone droning of the multiplication tables which is at the root of the trouble. This one has to check with all vigour, in the mechanically chanted tables the resultant number often comes out about a third lower in pitch than the rest, so that in "6 times 7 is 42", the lower-sounding 42 produces a mixture of complacency and pathos. This is no guarantee, however, that the children know the tables. It can happen that a whole class sing-songs through several totals in succession, all incorrect, until perhaps some child more alert sounds the alarm and wakes up the rest. And how boring even the most beautiful poem can become if a class or an individual lets the end of each line fall flat to the ground.

Special verses which are made up of long and short lines and, to some extent, move in free rhythms, will help to make the breathing as lively and flexible as possible; of course they are not in any way suitable for children below twelve or fourteen. One might think that children who, for several years, have gone through a conscious training of their breath would not need to have their breathing taken in hand again when they reach this age. The necessity for this arises from the onset of puberty. At this time the boys, in particular, fall strongly into gravity and, however loudly they are able to shout amongst themselves, hold the voice back completely when reciting: one must on no account reveal oneself! It is different with the girls: their forthright utterances are also more or less intended to prevent anyone else from looking too closely behind the screens they set up around themselves for concealment. For both boys and girls speech-formation just at this stage of development offers few attractions; they would rather give it a miss. However, if one denies them all possibility of hiding themselves and withdrawing into non-participation, one can, with some effort, get amazingly good results; in the end the children will themselves become enthusiastic when they experience how their speech is developing as an artistic instrument. Two verses may be given here with free, varying rhythms:

9.   As every organ within the whole must unite
           In service living,
           Good health to maintain,
           Must man in fellowship's weaving find his delight,
           In selfless giving,
           To strive ever fain.

10.   What into darkness has fallen
           Raise to the light! –
           Mithras when only a boy
           Swings himself on to the bull.
           Victor, finds he the way then
           Into Helios' realm.

The Healing Power
of the Vowels

The vowel is something which comes into operation
deep within the inner being of man; it is formed more
unconsciously than is speech in general. In the vowel
sounds we are dealing with intensely intimate aspects of
speech; what comes to expression in them is something
that belongs to the very essence of the human being.*

It is immediately obvious that, along with rhythm, the
individual sounds of language, vowels and consonants
alike, have great significance for anyone wanting to
heal with the help of the word. One only needs to
remember the fact that the very first sounds a baby
makes can often be characteristic for its whole life. A
little girl, for example, as soon as she awoke, repeated
perhaps twenty or thirty times over the same series of
sounds, *arulla, rulla, rulla, ru,* while her brother, born
a couple years later, lulled himself to sleep with *ababa,
aba, aba, ab.* This sequence of sounds was also repeated
over and over again. While the lullaby of the brother
became less clear and less articulated, however, the
awakening-call of the his sister, sustained throughout

* *Speech and Drama*, page 32.

37

by a rolling *R* with the tongue, finally became more and more energetic, and broke off like a short, vigorous trumpet-blast. Thus the choleric impulse to action and the phlegmatic comfortableness of sister and brother respectively came unmistakably into view in their first favourite sounds. Watchful observers of little children will recall similar examples out of their own experience.

I would like to come back again to the sanguine-nervous girl in my first class, who had such a peculiarly high-pitched, rather shrill way of speaking. In the lectures *Creative Speech,* Rudolf Steiner made a distinction between hearty "blood people" and often over-hasty "nerve people". The former have a full-toned speech which mainly depends on the vowels *A* (ah), *O, U* (oo) and *Au* (ow), whereas "nerve people" often make use of *I* (ee), *E* (as in "late") and *Ä* (approximately as in "fairy"). Attempting to work with nerve types such as this girl, using the Hahnemann homeopathic principle, I not only used the transition already indicated for such a case from anapest to iamb, but sought to base the verse on a picture which rayed forth tranquillity; and in my choice of words to find the way over from "nerve-sounds" to "blood-sounds", that is from *I, E, Ä* to *A, O, U, Au.* This kind of enterprise was often so difficult – especially when, besides everything else, particular consonants or consonantal sequences, on grounds to be explained later, had to be considered – that I often felt as if I was in chains and not able to fulfil every relevant condition. In the following verse an attempt was made to find a picture corresponding to the sanguine, the "airy-fairy" child.

11. As the wind speeds the glittering waves o'er the bay,
    And the eddying mist in swift dance sweeps away,
    As it cleanses the air till all clear is the blue,
    So it bowls our good barque on its course straight and true.
    The powers which tasks fulfil you'll too achieve,
    If your whole heart to light-filled aims you give.

An extremely ponderous phlegmatic child, almost bordering on the pathological, had a full, heavy speech which was given entirely to the blood-sounds *A, O, U.* As he usually arrived at school still half-asleep, despite a pretty long journey from home, he articulated so little one had a job to understand anything he was saying. It seemed urgently necessary to bring clarity into his speech, indeed to penetrate it with light throughout, and by means of *V* and *L* to give it some movement and flow. Out of such considerations I wrote the following verse:

12.   Gloom of night at last is going:
            Purple, gold and purest rose
            Sends the sun, a gift bestowing
            Ere his own bright face he shows.
            Gleeful the birds troll and twitter away,
            Seeing him rise and make lovely the day,
            Pouring forth life, and waking the will
            Duty in all things with love to fulfil.

In the Dramatic Course, after speaking about the individual sounds, Rudolf Steiner has a passage where he says: "In the sounds of speech live divine beings, and we must approach these beings with devotion, with prayerful devotion. They will then be the very best teachers we could possibly have."

Everyone who gives themselves to the cultivation of speech with some feeling of responsibility can confirm this. When they have successfully written a verse they are often astonished how some fundamental of speech suddenly dawns upon them to which they had given no thought during the actual work, and which perhaps had, up till then, even been completely unknown to them. This gives them an inkling of what high beings are connected with speech and whom they are petitioning to help in the work of education. Out of such a mood of piety and reverence they win the courage to continue serenely on the way they have begun to tread.

A young girl with a really happy disposition fell seriously ill when well past her seventh birthday, various functions of her normal metabolism breaking down simultaneously. After some time without the disorder being fully cleared up, she came back to school. She had looked forward to this with great eagerness, but her old freshness of heart seemed to have completely disappeared. Indeed, it could be seen that, instead of gradually getting better, she was in fact becoming ever paler and more exhausted; according to the doctor there was no physical reason to account for this. So I visited her parents and in the course of our conversation found out that during and after her illness, the child had been plagued by the sight of figures who came crowding out of every shadow and dark corner and filled her with fear. In the middle of the day, in the contrast between sunlight and shade, it was not so bad, but in the early morning as well as when the day declined, the experience became increasingly oppressive. The girl now fell into such anxiety and fear as bedtime approached that, evening after evening, her mother no longer knew how to quieten her.

In the street where the child lived there were plane trees growing, and as I was going home the evening sun was shining through their wide-spread branches. On the trunks, with their lighter and darker patches of bark, the sun was inscribing a flickering pattern as it shone through the leaves; on the ground also circles of light were criss-crossing each other. I took my start from this picture for making a verse for the girl, and turned to the light-filled *I* (ee) and the sun-sound *Au* (ow) for their help in healing. And so the following verse arose:

13.   The Sun – seest thou
               Where it limns bright
               Disclets of light?
               Heaven's blue – now
               Greets it not thee,
               Loving and free?
               Look! 'tween the boughs
               How the sun rays!
               Hear what it says!
               "Trust now arouse!
               Naught thee affright?
               Good is the light."

A fine late summer came to our aid. The girl soon began to love her verse beyond everything else. Her mother described how, when the critical time of late afternoon arrived, she would ask to say the verse together with her mother. Not long afterwards she wanted to see the light and leaf pattern beneath a nearby tree, and within a short time all anxiety had vanished. The more interested the child became in the play of the sun and shade, the more as a matter of course she recovered from her apprehensions and fears, and very soon with refreshing nights of undisturbed sleep she returned to her former good health.

The concentration of the sun-sound *Au* and the light-filled *I* (ee) was used in the same way to help another pupil, who was seriously out of balance in his whole being. His verse went like this:

14.
> Mysteries profound can tell
> The world to him who'd hear.
> Rouse thy wonder, listen well,
> Still be, deep revere.
> God did build the rounded sky,
> Blue – how blue! – above,
> And the countless stars on high,
> Showering down their love.
> Widen out, my soul, be still,
> Still as heaven's blue.
> Angels from their founts will fill
> Me with life's fresh dew.

A boy about nine had other difficulties altogether. He likewise became increasingly pale and shadow-like, but also more nervous and restless than before. As he was a strapping choleric, he became a veritable terror to the other children, a regular class tyrant. On the other hand, he was plaintively oversensitive about himself. When I visited his parents, which because of the father's work I could only do easily in the evening, nothing at first emerged which could explain the extraordinary change in the boy's nature. Then suddenly a terrible scream came from his bedroom. With wide-staring eyes and distorted face, the boy was cowering, all huddled-up, in a corner of his bed, as if seeking protection behind his pillow. He did not wake up, however, even when being put back to bed with comforting words. After a few uncontrolled movements with his head, he quietened down and went on sleeping, with beads of sweat still on his forehead. During the same evening he had two more attacks.

He had been born in really dramatic circumstances, for he came into the world during one of the worst air raids of the war. As it was the first time so fearful a bombing had been experienced in the area, there was something of a panic among the very people who had come to help his mother in her labour. There were also a series of other avoidable mishaps and it was lucky nothing worse happened, for it could have cost both mother and child their lives.

That in so early and decisive a moment of life an evil seed can be sown which can then come up years and even decades later, every experienced pedagogue will confirm. Especially in the ninth to the tenth year, and also in the twelfth, children go through decisive crises, when an old wound in the soul can open up again with sudden violence. Before the child takes leave of the spiritual world to seek its further development in an earthly body, it has around it in purity and harmony the helping activity of the spirit-beings in the starry worlds. It doesn't take much imagination to bring home how terrible must be the shock when, on the departure from such worlds and beings, the chaos and destruction of a bombing raid, of anti-aircraft guns, of burning cities and distraught human beings, of death and annihilation in every form, break in. Souls who have suffered this kind of experience in drawing their first earthly breath are liable to forfeit all faith in existence and to overreact to any negative condition in utter despair.

The boy needed energetic help from the school doctor because the damage was so deep within his whole organism. The teacher sought also to come to the aid of the child, with a verse. It was joy to him to hear that the boy had hung this verse, beautifully written out, over his bed and was saying it every morning with great devotion before coming to school. It goes without saying that this verse also had to be tuned to the blood-sounds.

15.　　　　From blue profound the stars look out,
　　　　　Where rests my heart with God at home.
　　　　　When golden dawn puts dark to rout,
　　　　　Then down to body's house I come,
　　　　　God's truth around goodness to impart
　　　　　To all I do with joy at heart.

In every class two types of children are to be found who cannot simply be grouped according to temperament, although their basic characteristics are bound up with temperament. Happy children, of course, will be essentially sanguine, but it is a different thing when children are merry and given to joy than when they are merely ready to laugh and be silly at every turn. Such superficiality, which through giggling and tittering can destroy a great deal for the teacher in any lesson, is not only to be found among adolescent girls, although among them such a tendency is strongly evident. It is just as bad if there are some representatives of the opposite sort in the class. There is the kind of child who has no real sense of humour: these children react sourly when they think they are not being taken seriously enough. They are mostly recruited from the ranks of the melancholics, but represent an unhealthy tendency away from the normal temperament, as do the over-frivolous among the sanguines. It is an even more serious matter if the humourless child feels called on to keep watch and ward over the moral sobriety both of comrades and teacher.

This kind of child one can only change through the gentlest touches of humour. Woe betide, however, if they catch on that one has them in mind! Then the game is lost. If, however, one can give the over-light of heart a verse with a gentle mood of *U* (oo) in it, the moralist must be led somewhat into *Ü* (a sound between "oo" and "ee" that has no corresponding English sound) or *Ö* (as in "fur").

16.   When in game upon game
                  Our first strength we exert,
                  And our heart sets an aim
                  For our will, then we start,
                  Truly brave, with trust filled,
                  For the future to build.

Only in the last two lines, where the dark mood of *U* is conveyed in "truly" and "future", is a more earnest note sounded. The morality-censor must be handled rather more drastically. Here one can point to the highest authority, to the Creator himself.

17.   When the great world was completed,
                  And the quiring angel-throng
                  God the Lord with praises greeted,
                  Festive, earnest in their song,
                  Words of goodness then God spake:
                  Joy the spring flowers doth awake,
                  Stirs the heart that it takes wing,
                  And 'gins jubilant to sing.
                  Beauty wheresoe'er it goes
                  With full hands itself bestows.

A quite specially strengthening influence is exerted by *E* (eh, as in "ate"). It is undoubtedly of great significance that in the language of ancient India, spoken when people still perceived the inflowing of the gods with reverent wonder, the *A* (ah) sound predominated. Today in our speech, *E* has taken its place. It induces people to lay hold of the earth with confident effort, as citizens of earth and no longer as exiles from heaven. Those who have difficulty in coming fully down to earth must at least be able to find consolation and support in looking up to heaven, and to feel some intimation of their angel as it blesses and protects them, as it were, from behind. The following verse is intended to help a child of this nature.

18.   'Tis man alone can pace erect,
            The hands can freely raise;
            Amazed can gaze at heaven star-decked,
            The good essay always.
            Thus aye he goes with steadfast stride,
            His loving angel at his side.

This verse accompanied a boy throughout the fourth year of school, so he was already older than nine years of age. That is an age when children no longer want to hear about heaven and the angels; a lot of tact is needed if one is going to speak about such things. What can be balm to the soul of one can provoke another to indignant rejection.

I have always found it interesting to see how early-maturing children accept it when a verse is given to a classmate which takes account of the latter's still childlike nature. On the other hand a kind of protection society is at once set up for anyone to whom, out of inadequate understanding, one has given a verse which is too young for him. Such an "insult" is rejected with one accord. On the other hand a verse will be well received that does not quite match the present condition of the child but does, with some real power, take hold of what is still resting in the future, even if this seems at the time to be altogether premature. Here is to be seen whether the teacher can be – as Rudolf Steiner puts it – a true prophet.

Nothing could be more beautiful than what happened in the fearful years of the Second World War when a young man just out of hospital and having endured unspeakable hardship and suffering, or a nurse just come from the death-bed of a brave soldier, wrote a few lines to say how a verse or story had been a help and a comfort in a moment of greatest stress. In a similar case a former pupil could find his peace in dying through the words of one who, as a girl, had been in the same class, and who as his nurse could help him to make the step over the threshold; for her, as she told me later, it was thus far the greatest experience of her life.

Three verses now follow which, in the way described above, will only fully unfold their meaning in the child later on:

19.   Where the heart's deep depths are set,
Let the lamp of God be lit:
In the head, where thoughts are weaving,
Let the sun's warm life be living.
And pure love glow through, reviving,
All thy seeing, doing, striving.
When, thus still, we serve within,
Enters HE, at first unseen,
Our friend, whose light lifts night's dark ban,
And makes us truly into man.

20.   One who is learning asks the master
How he is able to mount ever higher,
Though he has no one ever
To lead him.
He replies:
I do but listen, do but serve,
Become thus rich through giving;
His steps thus follow without swerve,
Who leads from death to living.

21.   Of Thee, love's source, we seek the sight
In beast and tree and stone,
In light of day, in blue of night,
In all and every one.
O find each heart with opened gate,
Go in, thence ne'er remove,
And let at all times consecrate
Each heart itself to love.

How Repetition Works

In a conversation with Rudolf Steiner the question once cropped up of what could effectively be done to combat poverty of feeling. Particularly with children in the big cities at the beginning of the 1920s, there could often be found a great coldness in their feelings, or even worse, a misdirection in them. Besides this, the will also could be enfeebled or distorted into brutality. Rudolf Steiner's answer was the simplest imaginable.

> The repetition of the beginning of a line has a good effect on the feeling, though what is repeated must have some significance. The repetition of the end of a line, of its last word or words, at the beginning of the next strengthens the will in a quite extraordinary way.

This indication one finds in a rather specialised form in what he says about feeling and will in *The Study of Man*.

> Thus more unconscious repetition cultivates the feeling; fully conscious repetition cultivates the real, actual will-impulse, for by means of it the power of decision is enhanced. And this power of decision, which otherwise

remains in the subconscious, is stimulated when you have the child do certain things again and again.*

Religious poets of the baroque period very often used repetition at the beginning of lines, for instance, in the words of chorales. To write verses for children which meet this requirement is not difficult; on the other hand, I found the sustained repetition of the end of one line at the beginning of the next without a cramping effect not at all easy, and consequently was successful with it only on rare occasions. Rudolf Steiner once made such a verse, which can help people who are weak or ill to activate their will in the best way possible.

22.
O Spirit of God, fill Thou me,
Fill Thou me within my soul:
My soul, to it give forces strong,
Forces strong also to my heart:
To my heart, that for Thee seeks,
Seeks with deepest longing:
Deepest longing for new health,
For new health and courage:
Courage, that in my limbs goes streaming,
Streaming as noble gift of God:
Gift of God from Thee, O Spirit of God.
O Spirit of God, fill Thou me.

My attempt to work in a strengthening way upon the feeling, according to the first suggestion, produced the following verse:

* *Study of Man,* page 6.

51

23.   'Tis love alone can heal the Fall,
             'Tis love gives all for naught,
             'Tis love that weds man to the all,
             Warms through my deed and thought.

A verse according to Rudolf Steiner's second piece of advice, composed to help a young man to take hold of what he was saying with more responsibility and control and to treat the word with more reverence, went as follows:

24. The soul of man from the breath of divinity springs,
    Springs forth from the gods' all-creative words,
    Creative words by the wafting spirit swift-winged,
    Swift-winged for the quest that leads to the heavenly portals,
    Portals which open the wrestling soul of man,
    Of man when his word is purely in service of God.

An indication of Rudolf Steiner's of quite another sort will serve to conclude this section. "Take care that a point of rest arises from time to time in the lesson. Look back briefly on what has already been brought forward, for this strengthens the personality and arouses the will to a fresh and more conscious effort." With this in mind I have occasionally given children verses I hoped would have a healing effect on their unsteady, disconnected natures. For such children, hounded and harried by one sudden notion after another, I tried to insert a point of rest into their verses, following with what had been indicated. Two examples will illustrate this:

25. As the onstreaming blood pulses forward in haste
    To the heart, that it there may find wisdom in rest,
    Must the soul to its own inner place e'er return
    If aught of creation through thinking 'twould learn.
    For whoso trusts the power within,
    Strength for his life as man shall win.

26.   As ended each creation day,
             God did His works review.
             So likewise you first work away,
             Then step back, and now you
             Ask, "Is't done well, or is't done ill?"
             If not so well, try harder still!

How the Consonants Help

One comes most readily to consonants and how they work by considering alliteration. Ordinary rhyme is melodic through its similar line-endings, and because it depends so much on the vowels it creates an intensive connection with feeling. In the same way, alliteration gives a strong impulse to the will. We know that the Teutonic warrior-hosts of old shouted alliterative battle-cries as they rushed to the attack. When these were roared forth from thousands of hoarse throats, magnified in a roll of threatening thunder behind the uplifted shields, the courage of the enemy had often ebbed away even before the battle had been joined, and many a conflict was already decided before it had even begun. Here indeed the primal power of the will was mightily at work in the speech.

When the ninth year is past and the fairy tale in all its delicacy can no longer carry the soul upwards, when the step of the foot begins to sound hollow and cold on the earth, and in inner anxiety children ask their teachers from where they draw their stability and certainty in life, it is time for alliteration to intervene with its helping forces. I have given many children alliterative verses over a period of two or three years. One must see, of course, that these verses are spoken with the necessary vigour and exertion of will, but on no account should there be any shouting by the children. Their speech by now should already have been well enough cultivated for there to be no danger of that.

27.   Timidly tender,
        Sprouts the seed,
        Helped by heaven in its need,
        Thrusts up and thrives,
        Stretches and strives,
        Braced 'gainst the blast,
        Strong and steadfast.

28.   Odin, the wisest of all who far wander,
        Took on great toil and great trouble undaunted.
        Gained he aught good, he gave it to others:
        Blessing is born, knew his heart, of such bounty.

29.   Gripping the ground with grasp of its roots
        Strong the tree stands, steady in storm;
        Foliaged boughs, reaching out far,
        Shelter and shade let all creatures share.

A first indication of the effect of consonants was with reference to *B*. Rudolf Steiner said children have "too little skin". "They everywhere feel a soreness where they meet the world and other people. That necessitates a great deal of *B.*" This prompted the following verse:

30. Mid boughs of the birch and the beech embowered,
    The birds build nests for their broods:
    With busiest care they bring up their babes,
    And warble their bliss through the woods.
    Go forth, thou brave child, and a strong castle build,
    Guard well there thy spirit's gold!
    Great blessing to grace it thy angel will give,
    And a shelt'ring hand o'er thee hold.

A verse with such an abundance of labial sounds as this however has quite another effect as well. This can easily be seen if one compares the first four lines with the last. Whereas the first lines have a lightly lyrical-poetic tone, in those which follow a gentle influence is exerted on the will, particularly through the *G* sounds (in go, guard, gold, great, grace, give). This began consciously with the *G* in go.

It therefore becomes obvious that one can give children who have something prosaic about them, or who have too little love and perhaps no trace of nest-warmth around them, such verses as this with labial sounds in them to a greater extent than usual.

31.   His shining flax with fingers deft,
             His web of finest warp and weft
             He spins and spools and weaves with skill,
             Who springs to work with all his will.
             Who weaves life's web with sun-bright thread,
             His path with joy will ever tread.

The many breath sounds or aspirants, especially *F* and *V,* also give warmth to the stream of speech as a whole. About this Rudolf Steiner said, "this expresses itself in the element of fire. Accordingly all breath sounds go over into the element of fire or warmth, when with feeling we bring out *H, Ch* [as in Scottish "loch"], *Sh, S, F, V;* all these live in the element of warmth." What is lacking in nest-warmth is gradually balanced out for the child, as it comes to be inwardly warmed by the fire-element in the speech.

We have a similar example, in which the lyrical element comes clearly into view, in the following small verse. In it the breath sounds give way to the labials *B* and *P.*

32.   The meadow flowers a-blowing
        Reflect the Sun's bright rays;
        A crown of beauty glowing
        They weave before my gaze.
        How blest my work shall prove,
        Bring I to it such love!

In *H* we have a breath sound which is often able to awaken animation and enthusiasm in the soul straight away. The *amphibrach* rhythm (˘ – ˘) gives a special support to this.

33.   When light from high heaven
            My heart is o'erflowing,
            Its young powers are given
            Such help for their growing,

My whole work at length
Wins beauty and strength.

Sh and *S* – the serpent sounds – on the other hand bring the human soul through conscious practice of them into a stronger bond with its earthly tasks. There was one boy who was quite unable at first to find his way properly down to earth. It could be seen from his delicately formed, almost angelic features – they reminded one of a girl's – that at heart he was for ever fleeing from the earth and longing for heaven. He had to learn that with heaven now behind him it was his task here and now to make himself at home on the earth. This was made the more difficult for him by occasional illnesses and accidents, which actually threatened to bring his life to an untimely end.

One year his verse went thus:

34.   From the stars thyself now sever,
            Seek creation's sense on earth;
            Be it shade or shine, seek ever
            Earth's true goal with strong endeavour.
            Solely thus win deeds their worth.

For a rather older child, whose characteristics were fundamentally the same without coming to such obvious expression, the following verse was made:

35.   God's world to me speaks words profound,
            In shine of sun and stars they sound,

Through splendours never ending.
True love for them they stir in me,
For man and beast and stone and tree.
And so, from skies descending,
To serve the earth I'll loving learn,
That into shining star she turn.

The study of the breath sounds can finish with two verses which were made up for the most part out of this group of consonants. It is also common to both verses that their form was sponsored by the wish to appeal strongly to the will of the children; hence, especially in the first verse, the frequent use of alliteration.

36. Hurricane-hurled 'gainst the shore-dykes, the sea-waves
    Storm, hacking holes with sledge-hammer blows.
    Haste now to help and make good all this havoc;
    Rest but a moment, 'twill put all at risk,
    Who on life's way would play his full part,
    Strive must he ever, steadfast of heart.

37. Heavenly forces with fire all a-glowing
    Surge full of life through the hands and the heart,
    Bidding the senses to be ever going
    Wonders to see in the world's every part.
    They give the heart fire, the feet winged speed,
    With them to create through strong, skilful deed.

Special among the sounds of speech is the *L*. Rudolf Steiner says of it that it is strongly connected with everything flowing, we also call it the wave-sound. It lives in the watery and also brings speech into flow. If one detects a slight hesitancy in a child's speech, it is always advisable to pay attention to *L*. In this situation *L* is especially effective in freeing the speech when it comes at the end of a word. An initial *L* often leads over from movement into form, especially if an impact sound stands at the end of the word. As an example of this, Rudolf Steiner gave the word *Beil* (hatchet) and its reversal *Leib* (body). The first brings something compact into movement, whereas in the second a form is built out of something watery and in movement. Accordingly, when attempting to heal through speech one must be very clear in the conscious use of *L* as regards what particular *L*-effect one is aiming at. In the first of the following verses the intention was to bring the speech-stream from an initial stagnation into a liberating flow, and thus call strongly on the will of the child.

38.   Will I, can I do my tasks?
            Fill my sack with all life asks.
            Rich I'll be, and richer still,
            If I do my best I will!

In the next verse the aim was to use the *L* in such a way that in their activities such children should be led out of fluidity into form. In doing this or that task they were always dreaming, in their artistic work as well as in other things, never properly finishing anything but letting it drop half-way.

39.   Through the body laid to sleep
      Will new life lets stream:
      Through the soul that bravely strives
      Will lets sunlight gleam:
      With the might of lightning-flash
      Will wakes man from dream.

Just as Rudolf Steiner related the *L* to water he brought the *R* into connection with the air. He once said that when one consciously made stronger use of the *R,* one could release forces from out of the astral nature into a soul which would otherwise be difficult to activate. To achieve this I once made this verse for a pupil:

40.   Oh steer right well,
      Brave, firm of will,
      Sure of your course!
      Barren's the ground
      Here and around
      Of all resource.
      Rocks and reefs past,
      Thou'lt reach at last
      Realms overseas.
      Straight you'll begin
      Rich freight to win,
      Rich joy and peace.

The consonants having the strongest connection with the earth-element are the impact sounds *B, P, D, T, G, K, M, N.* The two last in this series are hardly experienced as impact sounds nowadays. If one goes back to the Greek alphabet, however, these two letters are called *mu* and *nu*. The impact character of the two sounds thereby becomes much more obvious than when we say *em* and *en*.

With children who have difficulties in coming to terms with the earth, one will always find some mistake or other in their management of the impact sounds. In conversation with me Rudolf Steiner once said,

> From the way children form the impact sounds you will easily be able to determine where their trouble lies. If it is in the will the palatal sounds *G* and *K*, but also *H*, *Y* (German *J*) and *Ch* (as in loch) will not be properly formed. If the feeling is not entirely in order, it will be very soon found in the labials *B* and *P*, and also in *F* and *V* (German *W*). Most frequently of all, however, you'll discover irregularities in the dentals *D* and *T*, but above all in the sibilants *S*, *Z*, *Sh*, which are formed in the same area; here the defect has to do with the thinking of the children. The way the *M* and *N* are produced can show you how the connection of the children's soul-spirit being with the bodily nature is constituted. A merely cursory sounding of *R*, *M*, *N* indicates that difficulties have arisen for a healthy process of incarnation.

In the course of this conversation Rudolf Steiner also pointed out that where, for example, there are irregularities in the sounds related to the teeth such as *S* or *Z* they can be most quickly put right by a vigorous practice of the other dental sounds to the exclusion of the weak ones. Only after practising *D* and *T* for a long time should a child who lisps be led over to saying the *S*. It is important to find out where the faulty *S* is being formed before trying to put it in its correct place. As often as not the tip of the tongue is not reaching as far as the teeth. This results in a breathed-out sound something like *Ch*. If however the tongue shoots too far forward a sound emerges resembling the English *Th*. It is a bad thing if the *S* is being formed by sending the breath-stream sideways towards the cheeks or past the eye-teeth or canines; one then often has to go on for years before seeing any results.

All these deficiencies, moreover, in pronouncing the *S* have increased in recent years by leaps and bounds. Whereas forty years ago there might be less than ten per cent of such cases in a class, they can rise these days in certain circumstances to thirty per cent or more. Indeed, there are now classes in which half the children are lisping. It is quite astounding that many children who at first were saying *S* quite properly suddenly – just prior to starting with school as well as during the first few years of school – begin through imitation to acquire lisping defects which can only be eradicated with a great deal of trouble. It is like a real illness of the times we live in. Very often it is the artistically gifted children who have this defect from the start, or eventually acquire it. One feels that they take flight into the softness of this sound because they shrink back from the sharp clarity of the properly spoken *S;* they prefer to linger a little longer in dreaming, rather than risk waking up too much. With adults it is not uncommon to find this sort of thing among artists who are afraid of losing their powers through clear thinking.

One has to awaken very strong forces of consciousness and always keep them awake if one is to achieve anything in this area. In the first of the following verses the teacher tried to draw the whole attention of the child to the one and only *S* in it – in "save" – raising his finger at least a line ahead of it as well as following with the most intense awareness.

41.

They may the thorn hedge break clean through,
Who brave and faithful their help give ever,
They may humble-hearted do all they've to do,
Who save the day from demon endeavour.
To work bravely faithful then I will go,
That good and beautiful it grow.

In the verse which follows, the *S* is again almost entirely avoided, not because the child could not say it or could do so only with difficulty, but because the *S* actually conceals certain dangers within itself. There are children with something unpredictable in their natures who often manage to destroy the mood in a class through some foolishness or by calling out during a story. These children need protecting a little from the perilous serpent sound of *S*. The snake also likes occasionally just to let out a hiss. It lies with the teacher to give such children, who have taken leave a little too soon of the peace of Paradise, something of the calming fullness and divine riches which they so much lack. It was out of such considerations that the following verse emerged:

42. Above, every night, mid the blue profound
    My angel guideth me true,
    Where quiet ruleth the whole realm around,
    Healing the soul like the dew.
    When I wake and am 'ware of the green world without,
    From heaven there cometh to me
    The call: up and work, and away with all doubt!
    Thy angel hath full faith in thee.

The insertion of so many *Au* (ow) sun-sounds in the rhyming words was also consciously done. A strongly peaceful influence issues from them, as also from the picture that was chosen. With a frequent and deliberate resort to *Au* and the avoidance as far as possible of *S*, the following verse came about in a similar way:

43.   In trust look thou to heaven unbounded,
            In trust to earth below:
            Open the heart in love deep-founded;
            With light thy work shall glow.

The following verse is built up strongly on the *M*. The aim here was to help the child to find the balance between the soul-spiritual and the bodily elements in its being.

44.   In reverent mood God's world I view:
           God's eye in mildness looks on me.
           On earth, round-domed by heaven's blue
           I strive that good my work may be.

A much younger child was given this short verse out of similar considerations:

45.   Brave my mood, clear thought my guide,
           As mile on mile I go:
           And if I meet a stream too wide,
           Some bridge God will me show.

Among the impact sounds the *N* perhaps touches the earthly domain most gently of all. Accordingly I thought I might use it with some frequency when forming a picture that would not too pointedly show an egotistically inclined boy the way he should go.

46.   Springtime flowers unfold to sight
           Overnight.
           New their treasure,
           New our pleasure,
           New the beauty nature gives.
           Spring's long past, but see you how
           Autumn fruits rejoice us now!
           Nature again lives but to give.
           Ne'er says Nature "'Tis my own,
           All this wealth,
           For me alone."

None she turns from her great feast:
All she nurtures, man and beast.

In the following three verses no one impact sound is pre-eminent, but play is made with a whole set of them. The three children concerned – each of them a phlegmatic – found it difficult to come into action.

47.

Mountain pool,
Calm and cool,
Mirrors clear and fine
Stars aloft,
Moonlight soft,
Sun by day a-shine.
Torrents dash,
Foam and splash,
Over rock and stone,
Full of play,
Casting spray,
Finest veil, wind-blown.

Gently misting spray, its boon
Freshen all the plants outspread;
Gratefully the sun at noon
Paints the droplets green and red.
Till aloft a rainbow stands,
Traced as if by angel-hands,
And it tells to hearts aware:
"The world, life-streaming, is so fair".

48.   Forth creeps the snail from his round hut:
              Laughs the gnome till aching,
              Seeing how slow he moves his foot.
              "What a time you're taking!
              Do it thus! with will set to!
              Ponder not, but up and do!
              Ere you know you have begun,
              You will find you've almost done."

49.   Deep the rock within
              Lies a jewel fine:
              Come, thy task begin!
              Free it that it shine!
              Come! with main and might
              Break the stony shell!
              Bring the gem to light
              'Twill reward thee well.

As palatal sounds, *G* and *K* have an obvious connection with the human will. Consequently, verses intended to activate it must frequently resort to them:

50.   A good smith works within my will,
              Who for my sake with wondrous skill
              Shapes well my life in every part;
              I can him trust with carefree heart.
              Rare gifts through him to man are given
              By the good guiding powers of heaven.

The following verse likewise includes an abundance of palatals.

51.   God's gracious power
      Grows within like a seed,
      And comes to fair flower
      In every good deed.
      God's gracious light
      That within gently glows,
      There becomes bright
      And warm love bestows.
      God will me bless,
      If with good will imbued,
      Always I press
      To the true and the good.

While certainly less rich in palatals, the following verse is meant to spur on the will through its fire-kindling pictures and its measured amphibrachic (⌣ – ⌣) rhythm. It was made for a choleric.

52.   Brave, pure and light-filled,
      Heart steeled 'gainst the foe,
      Be each who'd, firm-willed,
      With Michael go.
      If his thought, word and deed be
      As done in God's light,
      A good sword will forge he
      As true spirit-knight.
      The dragon to conquer
      He'll strive without rest,
      The weak to make stronger
      Will be his high quest

> In combat unceasing
> Grim evil to thwart,
> Its captives releasing:
> That's ever his thought.

More strongly formed out of the palatals once more is the following little verse:

53. Who once the ground cleared, who the bull curbed for work,
    Who in care for earth's goodness no labour would shirk,
    A crownlet would win and great praise –
    Good work still ennobles these days!

We can conclude with the following verse, which was made for an older pupil. The boy in question on the one hand was intellectually gifted and had some depth to his nature. On the other hand puberty had brought the danger that his ability would tempt him to make superficial judgments, especially about those things he had earlier regarded as particularly valuable and even sacred. Thus there came about a verse built up entirely out of the dental sounds *T* and *D*. The intention was that the first lines should arouse an expectancy which in the fourth line would be followed by a surprising fulfilment.

54.   Step through the temple door,
       Treasure to guard.
       Holy it is, naught more:
       God's wondrous Word!

True be thou, let there shine
Through every word of thine
Bright gleam of light divine!
Enter, worthy, then the shrine.

Concluding Remarks

In a good many of my report verses it is not a question of a particular rhythm or this or that kind of consonant or certain vowels having been used. One of the first groups amongst these verses goes back to a particular recommendation of Rudolf Steiner's. Straight off in my first class there were two children, a boy and a girl, who struck me as being really slow-witted, whereas at home or when playing with other children they were far more lively. When I told Rudolf Steiner about this he said that in such a case karmic relationships would have to be taken into account. It was entirely possible that these two children were having to put up with a slow-witted nature in their present earth life as the karmic result of a lack of love in a previous one.

Generally speaking, it is important when teachers have such children in their class for them to try and find out who it was towards whom the lovelessness was shown in the previous life on earth. Astonishingly enough, the object of it will often be found quite close at hand. When a dimness of soul is discovered in two children in the same class, however, then it is quite certain that in the last life there was, between them, a mutual deficiency in love, perhaps even malice and underhandedness. If the educator could now bring them to actions of helpfulness and love towards each other, their whole being would begin to brighten up and their school work actually to show a distinct improvement.

Rudolf Steiner then gave a piece of advice which ran more or less as follows: you won't find it at all easy, however, to manage these measures. There are then two things you can try: on the one hand, give the children verses in their reports that are very much alike, so that each child is reminded of its own when the other is saying the one it has been given; in this way you set up the first conscious relationships. On the other hand, let one of the children, a boy for instance, do something for the whole class, such as looking after the flowers, and then talk to the other child, a girl, about it so that she can praise the other for his work and reliability. This must be followed up by the girl who has uttered words of praise doing something herself and the other in his turn expressing his appreciation. In this way you are building the first bridge between the souls of the two. And you will see how very soon the results will begin to come.

With the two children about whom I had asked for advice – they were in my class during the 1920s – the outcome was truly amazing, and in later classes of mine Rudolf Steiner's suggestions also proved completely valid.

Some examples of such verses shall now be given; while being very similar they also supplement each other, so that in some measure they fulfil the requirement specified.

55.   The stars in high heavenly spaces
                 In forms ever varied do shine,
                 Uncountable bright living traces
                 Of deeds done by beings divine.
                 And if with true heart I strive ever,
                 Light-filled will succeed my endeavour.

56.   Like the runes of a noble narration
                 Of doings in days long gone by,
                 In many a bright constellation
                 The stars shine down from the sky.
                 If devoted I strive with all power,
                 My being heart-warming shall flower.

The following is another pair of such verses:

57.   From heaven, where love-attended
                 We lived, all have descended
                 As brothers, sisters we.
                 On earth each sought the other,
                 That we might find together
                 True wisdom's treasury.
                 The light of worlds to view now,
                 Good work on earth to do now,
                 Bids spirit bravery.

58.   As sisters and as brothers we
                 To earth have all descended
                 From heaven, God befriended.
                 And now here in one company
                 Upon this good world do we gaze,

All standing still in deep amaze.
And when with spirit-bravery
We to our work do stride,
An angel will us guide.

The report verses must be suited to the stage of development of the pupils they are written for. Time and again Rudolf Steiner emphasised that the more pictorial a verse is, the more easily will it find its way into the child's understanding. If we concern ourselves with verses which Rudolf Steiner himself made for children, we may turn to the little verse which was given to the child in the third scene of the first Mystery Play, *The Portal of Initiation:*

Powers of light carry me
Into the spirit's house.

We find here a beautiful example of the pictorial language he refers to. Other verses of Steiner's for children seem to emphasise the thoughtful rather than the pictorial element, and we cannot but wonder if after all one has understood what he meant by the pictorial quality of a verse. His Angelus Prayer *(Abend Glockengebet)* has certainly got a thoroughly pictorial title, but the actual text seems to be more thoughtful in its tone.

59. To wonder at beauty,
Stand guard over truth,

Revere what is noble,
Resolve on the good.
This leadeth man truly
To purpose in living,
To justice in dealing,
To peace in his feeling,
To light in his thinking;
And teaches him trust
In the ruling of God,
In all that exists
In the widths of the world,
In the depths of the soul.

This verse, with such musical fullness in its rhythms, is one which younger as well as older children can live into completely. It is as if the picture of the bells, swinging and ringing so near to the heavens, were carrying the children, whatever their age, into the heights whence such wisdom-filled words were themselves sounding forth. What weighs on the teacher is whether he himself will ever manage to grow into such spiritual imagery.

At the end of a seventh year of school I gave two children verses in their reports, the first of which seems to me more pictorial, the second of a more thoughtful character.

60.   Kindle, tend the fire of will,
Till there melts the heavy slag.
Then what flows forth, pure and noble,
Shines out bright, like gold and silver.

61.   Every look into nature divine
          Calls us to fathom her depths.
          Every look into man's soul-being
          Wakens true love in our hearts.
          God's supreme sway ever weaves through the all.
          In doing be man the crown of creation.

From 1935 under the Nazi regime, the Waldorf Schools throughout Germany were forbidden to take any more children, and were eventually all closed down. In Wandsbek we accommodated more and more classes of the special school as our own classrooms became free. The result of this was that we came to be thought of as a school for children with intellectual and moral deficiencies, and for some years after our reopening in 1946 this image lingered on. And despite all our precautions in acceptances, we found ourselves at times with very difficult children in all our classes.

I had a youngster in my fifth class who was alert and lively and who at first seemed to have no special problem. Then one day I was going for a walk and came to one of the most desolate of the bombed-out areas in Hamburg. By chance I happened to look towards the remnant of a house whose lobby was still standing, and caught sight of my pupil looking round apprehensively from out of the empty doorway, and vanishing again. I went over and found some half-demolished steps which brought me down to a cellar which was nothing less than a thieves' hide-out. There he was, this pupil of mine, the leader of a youthful gang of robbers! Along with a pile of articles I even found a sum of several thousand marks.

I assured him that I would protect him from his accomplices, but he would have to decide at once whether I was to report the matter to the police or whether with my help he would return the stolen goods to their respective owners. After some struggle with himself he went with me to restore the money to the shopkeeper from whose till it had been taken. The latter was so delighted that he was prepared to give the young thief a finder's reward! I got him to refrain from this of course and instead to write out a receipt for the money returned. As we completed each difficult booty-restoring expedition, the lad showed obvious signs of relief, and in ever greater measure trust and gratitude bloomed forth in his heart. On the third or fourth day after my unexpected discovery he was going about with me on our final journeys with his face positively radiant. He was particularly happy at my not telling the class anything about what had happened.

During this time we were planning a more extended class-expedition than usual, for which money had to be collected, tents borrowed and ration-coupons arranged for. How astonished was my little robber-captain, when I put him in charge of all these things! It went better than it ever had before. Even the boy's father approved of what I had done in the end, though at first he had declined all responsibility if anything amiss happened through my rashness.

It now became a question of building up some moral responsibility in the child. It must be said again that apart from the parents, no one ever heard anything from myself about all this, so that no suspicions were aroused in the class through the following verses.

62. Deep hid, as if only of rock dull and grey,
    Lies the ore of your good will below.
    Quarry it out and bring it away!
    And bright in the fire let it glow!
    Tend it, and never you mind how you sweat!
    Work with all main and all might!
    For look at the bright shining silver you get,
    If good faith with your work you unite!

63. Around in a whirl the frothing foam races,
    In water a-seething roll sand-grain and stone.
    There's glitter of gold in those pale-green spaces,
    Then in gravel swirling all sight of it's gone.
    You scoop up handfuls from depths swiftly flowing,
    Then pebbles and sand you wash clean away:
    And see! the grains left are pure gold a-glowing,
    Which homewards you bear, your heart gratefully gay.

The contact which the lad came into with myself as treasurer for our camping enterprise proved of the greatest value for him. Because of it we could speak of his verse together on several occasions. When he left school and began his work training, the confidence which had developed between us continued, even long after he was qualified.

When Rudolf Steiner had met the Waldorf School teachers in September 1924, shortly before his last illness, he had promised to give some lectures about the contact necessary between teachers and pupils who had moral difficulties. He had wanted thereby to address what had concerned him at the three previous college meetings, and about which he had actually intended to hold a seminar course for the teachers. He indicated what he considered essential in cases of extreme moral danger. "In such cases admonitions, discussions about moral issues are useless. The only thing that helps is such a connection to the teacher that the pupil feels a special attachment to him, feels specially drawn towards him."*

We have to proceed with kleptomania in quite another way. Rudolf Steiner also spoke about this in the July meeting:

> Where you have to do with kleptomania the position is really like this: the human being has two contrasting, polar organisations, the head organisation as one of them having the basic tendency to appropriate everything; it simply has to take everything for itself. The other pole, the metabolic organisation, is the bearer of moral experience. One could actually make a diagram of the situation by drawing a lemniscate. The head-organisation does not recognise property-rights; it only recognises its own absolute right to whatever comes within its reach. The other pole recognises the moral factor. When the head organisation slips down and enters the will-organisation, kleptomania is the result. It is an illness that arises when the elements proper to the head-organisation

* *Faculty meetings with Rudolf Steiner,* Vol. 2, July 15, 1924

are active in the will-organisation. Actual thieving is something entirely different from this. The disposition to kleptomania can be recognised by a marked absence of consciousness during the stealing: things are appropriated simply because they are seen. The actual object is the tempter, no finesse is practised in order to gain it.

A girl in one of my classes was constitutionally predisposed to kleptomania. Things vanished in an altogether mysterious way when she simply went past them; when called to the blackboard, for instance. She herself seemed to be amongst those most astonished when one extracted from some hidey-hole what she had let disappear into it. One could clearly detect the absence of mind which came over her when the enticing objects exerted their suggestive influence. Just how little the girl had any consciousness at all in her own hands showed itself quite obviously when she had to draw a human being. What she produced was a figure without any hands. When the teacher said that there was something missing in the picture which she must put in, she pondered the problem for some time, and gave the girl she had drawn a hat; and when this failed to satisfy her teacher, she added some buttons to the coat! The arms still remained as handless stumps. In her report verses accordingly it was a question of trying to awaken a stronger consciousness of the hands. The examples will make this clear.

64.   These hands, God-fashioned, are indeed
            A masterpiece divine;
            If them with skill I use, rich meed
            Of joy will then be mine.
            They build the house and bake the bread,
            Prepare the drink, and loving aid
            Give all in need, for so God bade.

65.   Once said the feet unto the pair
            Of hands: "Pray, may we ask
            You idlers – we who always bear
            The body – what's your task?"
            The left hand to the right straightway
            Said, "Brother, I serve you."
            The right however naught did say,
            But painted, wrote and drew.
            Naught else its maker imitates
            Save man's own shaping hand.
            Boldly, freely it creates
            Beauty's wondrous land.

Examples and Suggestions

In this chapter a series of report verses, which come out of forty-two years of class-teaching, will be given by way of example and stimulus. If anyone took the comfortable line of just appropriating them for their own use, they would have completely misunderstood what has been intended all along. A colleague wanting in this way to ease her work over her reports and report verses would inevitably rob herself of the blessing concealed in her own labour. The following examples aim to show how differently the task can be attempted. To finish with, some examples will be given of verses composed over a number of years for the same child.

In my first years as class teacher I was lucky enough to have only quite small classes, so that verses were needed for only a few children. It was not long, however, before even a first class came to have over fifty children in it. I often sat at a report and its verses for hours on end, and asked myself more than once whether such an expenditure of one's forces was, generally speaking, worthwhile. My experiences with the verses and the fruit they bore for the children taught me that none of the trouble I had taken was in vain. This is why I want to pass on to younger colleagues the suggestions given to me by Rudolf Steiner in the hope that they may be useful to them as well.

The first verse-metre which Rudolf Steiner turned my attention to was the choriamb (– ᵛ ᵛ –). Just this rhythm has something in it that kindles inner fire and awakens courage. At the same time it is often necessary with a very self-assured choleric to damp down the temperament a little. The first of the following verses was given with this in mind.

66.   Look! 'gainst all curb,
                Fierce, full of force,
                Foaming in rage,
                Rears up the horse.
                Canst hero be,
                Inwardly steeled?
                Seize then its rein!
                Hold till it yield!
                Then to the plough
                Harness straightway!
                As its own lord
                Thee 'twill obey.

67.   Faithful and free,
                Carry right through
                All you've to do:
                Fruitful 'twill be.
                If each endeavour's
                Bravely begun,
                Victory ever's
                Surely half-won.

With the trochee (– ᴗ), which has an awakening effect, one turns to children who need rousing a little out of their peace and quiet.

68. Mark yon fledgling, safely housed
In its cosy nest,
From its dreaming rarely roused,
Eating of the best
Thus 'twill grow and strength 'twill gain
Steadily each day,
Till no longer is it fain
Still at home to stay.
Off into the world 'twill fly
Lands afar to view,
Rich in heart, since valiantly
Thus it dared to do.

The following verses would be suitable for older children:

69. Through thy steadfast hand's creation
Thou the spirit's sword will fashion;
For on substance and on work
Highest wisdom leaves its mark.

70. Mother art thou, kindly earth,
Bringing countless seeds to birth.
Sunwards every plant is lifted,
Till with fairest flowers 'tis gifted.
Helping heavenly powers also
Stand near thee, with thee will go.

71.   God's own word did make the whole;
God's own breath the living soul
Gave to all, both high and low.
And the word divine doth flow
Into man's own song and speech.
Tend thou in love God's gift so rich.

72.   Strive I ever with brave heart,
Forge I thus the sword of spirit.
Great the joy I then impart
To my angel, and I merit
More the help he'd fain bestow.
Steadfast goalwards then I go.

We have a still more awakening rhythm in the dactyl
($-\,\smile\,\smile$).

73. Down in the dark, past the stone, past the gnome,
Murmur the streams as they flow through the gloom.
Whispering, runing of light full of wonder,
Onward they wind till the rocks part asunder.
Then into day where the tiny birds sing,
Shimmering bright into light flows the spring.
Lovingly gives she herself to each wight,
Quenching all thirst in unending delight.

Would I the beauty of earth e'er discover,
Ne'er must I shrink from thoughtful endeavour:
Would I myself ever beauty achieve,
Diligent work and all care must I give.

Love for the deed lend wings to my doing,
Then may I rest in God's love all-renewing.

74. Dances the wind o'er the waters a-blowing
One with the waves as they heave up and down,
Whirling about, now coming, now going.
Ocean in shimmering, billowing gown
Calls out to thee in its ebbing and flowing:
"Thou must create, wouldst thou win beauty's crown."

In the hexameter, which consists of six dactyls, with the two shorts sometimes compressed into one syllable, there lies the power not only to awaken the child's being, but also to get rid of stuttering and other speech hindrances.

75. World-swaying power in the wind wields the breath
of the Asa, great Odin,
Firing with flash of the lightning the heart with high courage undaunted:
Wafting o'er fields ever-waving, the wind is preparing
the harvest:
God's breath of blessing a picture becomes for
my heart's intimation.
Stream too through me, consecrating with
heavenly power ever-healing:
Wide be my heart as the world, so that God grace my word
and my working.

The iamb (ᴗ –) is the rhythm which particularly tautens and concentrates the being of the sanguine child.

76.   Be clear, my deed!
        Be pure, my heart!
        And as the sun
        True light impart.

77.   From heart's deep store take seed and sow
        Within the well-ploughed field.
        'Twill in the loving sunlight grow,
        A harvest rich to yield.

78.   "Let there be light!" God said, and lo!
        The whole wide world shone bright.
        And as a friend's God's face does show
        Wherever shines the light.
        If man true love will ever give,
        Warm, mild and filled with light
        Then as God's image will he live
        In sunshine ever bright.

79.   The breath of God lets stream in me
        The air my whole life long:
        Resound I make it, uttering free
        My heart in word and song,
        As prayer they come before God's throne:
        As joy men hear their every tone.

80.   How comes to be the whole world wide
        So good, so pure, so fair?
        God lets His gaze on all abide
        And keeps us in His care.

> And work we with full love and power
> At all tasks small or great,
> Then beauty from our deeds will flower,
> And angels jubilate.

Just as the dactyl in certain connections is an enhancement of the trochee, so the anapest (⌣ ⌣ –) can be regarded as enhancing the iamb.

81. As in winds a-wafting in time of the spring
Little birds wing their way from the South's sunny skies,
And make joyful our hearts as rejoicing they sing,
All a-shimmer with colour in bright-feathered guise,
Down we come everyone from the realms above
To the earth, with delight its beauties to view,
And creating together with deeds of true love,
Through the help of the Angels the world to renew.

82.   Never sluggishly still
                Be my thought and my will,
                But in deeds ever active and steady.
                Then must head and must hand
                Skill achieve, and thus stand
                As good servants, for work ever ready.

83. What of all the world's glorious beauty divine
Is revealed to your heart here on earth,
Clear and bright through every creation may shine
Which yourself on life's way bring to birth.

84. What within shines as bright as the power of light,
    What without ripens on into deed,
    May they both, as you seek to become a true knight,
    All your steps towards Michael lead.

In the following verse the anapest is used at the beginning, and the iamb more and more frequently towards the end. I often used this change of rhythm with children who needed to be led from a confused into a clearer-minded condition of soul.

85. Once Seaghan had trained his good steed to obey,
    Defeated, the dragon withdrew.
    And when men with sure hand o'er themselves hold sway,
    And with well-balanced thought weigh each sentence they say,
    Every fight they as victors win through.

86.   Foaming the waves roll in,
          Crashing with mighty din.
          Into them bravely dive!
          Strength will thy courage give.
          Fight thou, ne'er yield the way,
          Manful, win thou the day!
          Work thou right valiantly,
          Good all thy deeds will be!

The following verse begins with the iamb, and in passing to a shorter line tries to achieve a concentrating effect.

87.   To strive in earnest
         Through life thou learnest
         Aright,
         If head and will
         Clear aims to fulfil
         Unite.

The amphibrach (˘ – ˘) is an extraordinarily harmonising and at the same time fire-kindling rhythm. It is especially suited to melancholic or shy, withdrawn children.

88.   In light we are weaving,
         For beauty e'er striving;
         And always I would
         Do only the good.
         And angels, this viewing,
         Rejoice at our doing,
         And bless every one
         Who to work presses on.

89. The sun and the moon and the stars I love,
      Man too and the beasts, great and small,
      The pasture, the cornfield, the woodland grove,
      Earth, water, air, fire, each and all.
      With thankfulness warming my heart I'll live.
      In service of God all my days to strive.
      The Angels behind me, reveals my heart,
      See all I do and their blessing impart.

90. The earth with its stones safely bears me:
    In stones strength and goodness are hid.
    To plant, beast and man the world over
    They give the sure ground which they need.
    The earth and its rocks thus serve us,
    The beasts too and plants give us aid,
    And I will myself bear and cherish
    All creatures which heaven has made.

91. When within man beholds the heart's warming sun,
    And his deeds out of love come to birth
    And beauty and knowledge and goodness are one,
    Then he's a free being on earth.
    To noblest of aims his whole strength he gives;
    For them he will strive as long as he lives.

    I had a particularly remarkable case of speech difficulty to deal with in a girl who behaved in school as if she were mute. Before she came to us she was often rebuffed with "Keep still, you're just stupid." Because of this she had suffered a deep injury within the soul. I tried to help her with the following verse:

92. To Adam gave God, as Father of all,
    His breath, and thus did He speak:
    "Go, name me all creatures, the great and the small,
    The noble, the strong and the weak.
    For I, who created the world through the word,
    The word in thy speech on thee have conferred."

To another girl who was very gifted in drawing and painting but also had difficulties in penetrating into speech and shaping it clearly, I gave the following verses in three successive years:

93. Wondrously working the all-swaying word
    Worlds and their beings created,
    Out of its slumber the soul it then stirred.
    With bands of bright gold it united
    Man unto God through praise and through prayer,
    Sounding in worship and joy everywhere.

94.   Wielding word-power strong,
            People of past ages,
            So we learn, looking back,
            Spoke a speech creative.
            Courage, fire-enkindled,
            Out of hearts heroic
            Stamps the spirit's gold
            Anew upon word-power.

95.   As to earth the Logos came
            Down from where world-music sounds,
            Men's hearts entering like flame,
            Out of depths of soul was heard,
            Far within the temple-bounds,
            From mouth to mouth the holy word.
            If 'tis then to heal man's wounds,
            It must light, by spirit stirred,
            Deep in the heart a glowing flame.

In the first two of the following verses alliteration is used to strengthen the forces of the will. Between the ages of nine and twelve, alliteration often works splendidly in putting fire into children. A few examples of such verses run as follows:

96. In winds all a-whirl, with mighty steps wending,
    Far-seeing, deep-thinking, there seeks the All-Father,
    As wandering wisdom in hearts of true heroes
    Great aims to arouse in the ground of their being.

97. Whom the marvel-filled world to wonder can move,
    Who rouses himself to brave deeds without rest,
    Whose heart is illumined with light-filled love,
    To him, at the last, life's fruit will fall.

98.   Seek the sun-waters bright,
            Brave, active, free!
            Drink of their living light,
            God's gift to thee!
            Win, working lovingly,
            Michael's creator-might!
            Helper, protector, HE
            Leads us by day and night.

99.   In fire, scattering sparks abroad,
            To steel is changed the iron-stone
            Shaped to a share it cleaves the clod,
            That grain for daily bread be grown.

After the twelfth year one is often led to use repetitions, such as are formed so beautifully in Rudolf Steiner's verse, "O Spirit of God, fill Thou me ..." (verse 22), in such a way that the concluding words of one line became the first words of the following. Whilst with the younger children it is the sound-painting rhythmic quality of the alliterative repetitions that activates the will, in older pupils it is the impressive repetition of the words themselves.

100.   No goal you reach just standing still:
         Just standing still you lame the will.
         The will you strengthen through your deed,
         Your deed which gives to life new seed.

101.   Love awakens, wakens deeds:
         Deeds cry, "Up, and meet life's needs!"
         Alone who wills, wills with power,
         Sees with joy deeds come to flower.

102.   To Earth we're borne by starry forces,
         Starry forces of high heaven.
         In high heaven were they planted,
         Planted deep down in our will;
         In our will brave strength bestowing,
         That true, pure, good be all our doing.

For fear of betraying too much of their own soul-being, children who are actually very gifted artistically often, in their painting, take to laying ever paler colours on to the paper. In such cases I gladly turned in their verses to the three primary colours (or *Glanzfarben,* shining colours, as Rudolf Steiner called them).

103.   Shining yellow, red and blue,
                Kin of night and day,
                Show in dancing fro and to
                Hand in heart the way,
                So that what's born of semblance bright
                In spirit shines with beauty's light.

104.   Heart's devotion, full and true,
                Holds its sway in heaven's blue:
                Rev'rence for yellow's light sublime
                Shines beyond all space and time:
                Red flames up, red paler glows,
                Till there opens love's fair rose.

105.   In circling dance the colours bright
                Gently change my soul for me.
                Should their full beauty come to light,
                There the Christ will be.

In such a verse as the one that follows the experience of colour only sounds in as it were from the side.

106.   Joy in colour your own knowing
                Fashions into pictures clear,
                When thereby your heart's all glowing,
                Truth in radiance comes it near.

> Hearken! reverent, faithful, true,
> Then on wings thou'lt strive anew.

It is a matter of course to many children in the first and second classes that they have come down out of the heights of heaven. Many of these young companions only too quickly forget their heavenly home, however, and bid fair to enter the rigidities of earth before their time.

107.
> By God's light always tended,
> From heaven we've descended,
> Good brothers each to each.
> And each seeks out the other,
> That we may strive together
> Bright wisdom's source to reach.
> To see truth's light shine forth,
> To build on ground of earth,
> Love's courage this would teach.

108.
> What entered out of heaven's height
> My body, as its dwelling place,
> Is that which lives in me as light,
> And gazes out as human face.
> Keep I this house clean, clear and fine,
> Wakeful my spirit within shall shine.

109.
> My angel said his "Yes"
> To my life's way, and so
> Self-trust I'll bravely build
> On life thus angel-willed.

May all my doing show
That strong and clear I too say "Yes."

The following verses which speak of sun and stars are also meant to remind the child of its home in heaven.

110.　　　I gaze up at the sun with wondering eye,
　　　　　As in high state it rides across the sky.
　　　　　Down does it look on what the people do,
　　　　　Fain to rejoice at what it there may view.
　　　　　My angel too looks down in radiant light;
　　　　　If beauty I achieve, his face shines bright.

111.　　　How wakes the sun to birth
　　　　　Life through its radiance bright!
　　　　　What's rooted in the earth
　　　　　It wins up into light.
　　　　　Where work is a holy thing,
　　　　　Beauty itself bestows:
　　　　　Who'll joy to learning bring,
　　　　　Its glowing radiance knows.

112. The stars' twinkling glances, the sun's shining rays,
　　　The greening and blooming and fruiting of earth –
　　　These riches I welcome with joyful amaze.
　　　From the realms both of heaven and of earth sounds forth.
　　　To me, all expectant, a word full of fire:
　　　"Through art raise nature, O man, ever higher."

There now follows a whole series of verses which are formed out of pictures.

113.   World-riddles have their answers, friend,
        But hidden deep they be.
        Who'd find them out must, steadfastly
        To deepest depths descend.

114. Nightly the soul soars high into heaven,
        Drinks from the springs of the stars with delight
        Down to the earth it comes with the morning,
        Sets to and works with main and with might
        What first it glimpsed in the high realms above,
        It seeks here to fashion in beauty and love.

115.   Love's pledge ranks first in every land,
        Love consecrates both heart and hand.
        Would'st rightly see, would'st rightly do,
        Then build on love thy whole life through.
        It makes thee one with all for aye –
        'Twill open heaven's gate one day.

116. From India's wisdom which worshipped the One
        Had man at last to be banished.
        The warring Persians lost sight of the sun,
        For the men of the Nile the gods vanished.
        The heavens the Greeks felt around them on earth
        Now threaten to pass from our gaze.
        Wouldst banish decline and all its dearth
        Thou must strive to become, all thy days.

117.   Be wakeful, active, grasp all clearly!
        Dream not, nor be driven merely!

Only so your ship you'll steer
Of reef and sandbank safely clear.

118.   Great is the knowledge that sages feeds,
         Greater their counselling word,
         Greatest the helping, the loving deeds,
         Done without thought of reward.

The next three verses were to recall the forces and power of the word.

119.   In nature and in spirit realms
         What happens, works and forms,
         What rays and streams,
         What glows and gleams,
         What threatens, forces, harms,
         All skilled, man's word to action springs,
         And grasps them all aright:
         It freshly paints and draws each thing,
         And gives them spirit-light.

120.   In tone and sound the word can flower
         Where spirit-light is lit,
         And when 'tis shaped by heart's own power,
         And love speaks out of it.

121.   Bird-song making glad the day
         Ever to God's throne finds its way.
         And what men say and what men sing
         Into His heart can ever wing,

> If reverently they let be heard
> In their own speech His mighty word.

In the next three verses hands and feet are the leit-motif.

122.   All beings are filled with wonder to see
How man on his feet stands firm and free,
And to the Creator lifts hands in prayer,
And feels himself godlike whensoe'er
He too creates beauty. Then angels gaze
At the work of his hands in rev'rent amaze.

123.   See how head and senses rest
Cool and quiet up yonder.
They as picture teach us best
How listening we must ponder
World-questions in our mind,
If answers true we'd find.

124.   Clearest light man's thinking leads,
Loving light his feeling guides.
When they stir his hands to deeds,
Blessing on his work abides.

For the third and even on into the fourth year of school I have gladly made use of pictures to do with sowing, blossoming and ripening. Occasionally I have also referred to the creative forces which in winter prepare for the growth to come.

125. What's closely confined within the seed
     By water and light and warmth is freed;
     When they the seed-walls burst asunder
     Such beauty appears, all gaze with wonder.
     So free thou also and bring to light
     What in heart and mind now's hid from sight.

126. The soil must be loosened for green to grow,
     And water must stream if life is to thrive;
     And the air bring warmth for the flowers to blow:
     Thus when frost is past all things revive.
     If too in life's pulsing stream you'd mould
     Forms of beauty with love at heart,
     In trustful courage you need but unfold
     What in goodness to you the heavens impart.

127.   The tree braced firm 'gainst winds a-blow
         Is strong and good.
         Who masters hindrances does show
         True courage unsubdued.

    Pictures drawn from many sources come into the
next verses.

128.   Out from its hard case confining,
         Hid long for many a day,
         A wonder in colours all shining,
         The butterfly flutters away.
         Then bravely strive with all power;
         What you win from tasks great and small

From the soul full of light will flower,
A treasure of earth blessing all.

129.　　Carbon filled with light
Shines as diamond clear.
Who by the good and right,
Which they on earth hold dear,
Guide all the deeds they do,
Themselves grow light-filled too.

130.　　What I have is only loss,
If I give the other naught.
If I give in love, I go
On life's way most richly fraught.

If one intends to say something about laziness and diligence, one has to be specially careful not to play the philistine or the preacher.

131.　　How much effort, how much sweat
Gives the farmer ere he get
Recompense in harvest sheaves!
Who himself spares naught achieves.

132.　　Who o'er lethargy ne'er prevails
A slave must stay:
Along the road of life he trails,
Full oft astray.
Rouse into deed your slumbering power,
Lest deeper it sink from sight:

From hard, honest work alone can flower
What the heart will truly delight.

133. When radiant beauty transfigures the morn,
And the glories of noon the whole landscape adorn,
When the westering sun bids farewell and departs,
And God's love almighty flows into men's hearts –
If these see in me a hard worker good-willed,
At night will my angel stand by me joy-filled.

The following verses were meant to make demands
on the will and on the feeling of responsibility.

134.   Courageous, strong and loving ever,
Serving all with best endeavour,
Dedicated reverently
To all beauty, I will be.

135.   Who knows and who can must as well
Work, and shape life through his deeds,
Which then for the combat of spirit
Will forge him the weapons he needs.

136. When honest good-will sets the heart afire,
Right strong grow the wings of the soul.
And those who with love to the highest aspire,
All hindrance despite, reach the goal.
Them into light do their pinions lift.
With gold to be crowned, their angel's gift.

137.   Path-preparer for the light:
           'Tis as this my will I see.
           Forth into the spirit's fight
           Fresh each mom it summons me.
           Will not my angel lead me ever,
           Rouse I myself to full endeavour?

Rudolf Steiner referred to Goethe's saying, "What is duty? When one does what one tells oneself to do." He added to this, "We have to be brought to this, but we are only brought to it when there is present the sequence of gratitude, love and duty."* These words are the leitmotifs for work on report verses.

138.   Earth's duties each day
           With love to essay,
           Steadfast ever
           In noble endeavour,
           With strength, in brave mood
           To work – that is good.

139.   Every duty with love's fire
           Do, O man; then, past all doubt
           Nobler grows the heart's desire,
           Till the earth like sun shines out.

140.   From the heaven's blue,
           From the starry round
           Falls refreshing dew
           On to earthly ground.

* *Human Values in Education,* lecture 6.

> And the spirit's fire
> Warms the heart for the right,
> That it aspire
> To serve bravely the light.

141.   With his true deeds helps every man
       The earth to change its form,
       That so according to God's plan
       It can a star become.

142.   Change the darkness into light,
       Fire to powers of will:
       For know! the countenance of Christ
       Thou must thyself unveil.

Verses given to the same children over a number of years

A shy girl, who was always holding back and who, to begin with, was easily overlooked in class, received the following six verses one after the other. Slowly overcoming her phlegmatic temperament, she developed in a most delightful way.

143.   Through loving endeavour
       Do roses ever
       Grow from the ground.
       Angels unceasing
       Look down in blessing

From heaven's blue round.
And when through and through
Is done what's to do,
Their glad songs resound.

144.   Seek now the sun's deep spring,
Active and bold:
Gifts from God's hand you'll bring,
Shining like gold.
Power to work, power to give,
Michael both bestows;
Each day, each night with us
Guardian and help HE goes.

145. Who looks at the world with wondering gaze,
Who himself bestirs to brave deeds ever,
Whose heart lights up with love always,
Life's fruit wins at last through his endeavour.

146. If warmth, light-filled, in head is living,
And through the heart light, warmth-filled, flows,
If works the hand with skill and vigour,
Blessing the angel-world bestows.

147.   The wealth of the soul
Thou findest not,
Though wanderest thou
The whole world through.
Look out into space,
Thou findest the light,

Whence thine own soul
Once entered the world.

One after another in the course of five years I gave the following verses to a dreamy phlegmatic. He stands in life today active and productive, a mature man.

148.   Joyful work will always
            Lead by sunlit pathways
            Towards God's light unceasing,
            Towards the angels' blessing.

149.   Tranquilly the waters rest
            In the mountain lake,
            Till beneath the lofty crest
            Bravely they awake:
            They rush down the valley, a highland stream,
            The mill-wheel turning in circles unceasing.
            Who his own forces stirs up from their dream,
            In fruitful labour will win great blessing.

150. Who works with all strength, his own will bestirring,
            The gods hold dear and will richly dower.
            Thor blesses the farmer who, never once fearing
            The hardest of work, awakes his own power.

151.   The sun each spring within the earth
            Awakens life with growing power,
            From the seed plants come to birth,
            And from the plant the radiant flower.

Man wakes to work, and in his doing
His own good strength he feels a-glowing.

152. Stays yet the barque, though winds be blowing,
Held by moorings taut?
See how the sails yearn to be going!
Whither? To farthest port!
Steersman, all thy courage muster,
Brook no more delay!
Master be, though storm-winds bluster!
All will be well. Away!

A boy who had something of a real split in his nature and yet, one could hope, also had it in him to develop his positive qualities to the full, received the following six verses. When recently he brought them back to me I was amazed to see how magnificently he had overcome his difficulties during the many years since he left school.

153. The sun its light on me bestows,
My limbs' good strength increasing;
To work then does it call me forth:
I go, with joy unceasing.

154. God's breath creative streams in me,
Speech within me shaping:
God's eye in love it rests on me,
That truth be in my speaking:
God's strength glows warming through my blood,
Sure guide in my endeavour.

May all I do be true and good,
To evil I'll stoop never.

155. Heimdall of heaven. all-seeing, ne'er sleeping,
     Watches the world from Bifrost Bridge:
     Fierce giant foes, to destroy come they creeping,
     Forth the swift Asas he summons to fight,
     Fearless defending the fair city bright.

156.   A hero is he who in fair fight
            Is ready to defend the right:
            A coward skulks where none can see,
            Through craft he'd steal the victory.
            That which I am, may each one know:
            Brave, open-hearted ever I'd go.

157. The eagle circles towards the light,
        A king upon his way:
     No lethargy slows down his flight,
        All weight below must stay.
     Man's spirit, woven of sunrays fair,
        In sloth would sure decay:
     But striving up through light-filled air,
        All bonds it casts away.

158. God plants a seed in each heart deep
        Of good to be:
     But into the heart's blood there doth creep
        Man's enemy.
     You can the soul's good from his grip
        Through fight set free.

If you but dauntless courage keep,
Then die must he.

A boy who, on the one hand, was very finely con-
stituted, but on the other could fly into sudden rages,
received the following verses:

159. Beauty, my heart's love shows to me,
     Shines when all join in true harmony.

160. Whate'er's on the world's great wonder-tree
     Plays each its part. Lost aught there
     Its place, how small soe'er to thee,
     The rest would go for naught there.
     Know then with reverent, loving soul:
     The smallest dwarf helps build the whole.

161.   Thor, the giants hip and thigh
          Smiting, sees a foeman fly:
          Hurls his hammer, and cries he,
          "Mjölnir, my delight,
          Fell him, then fly back to me!
          Here I still must fight."

162.   Blinding rage will thwart the bull,
          Since its strength goes then for naught.
          Learn thy fiery blood to rule:
          Sun-bright then will shine thy thought.

163.   The birds anew their songs do sing
          Each year that comes and goes,

The leaves, the flowers return each spring,
The sea-tide ebbs and flows.
Sense from the world would soon be gone,
Ceased deeds creative ever,
And much of worth's already won
By each one's best endeavour.

164. Hid deep within a chest
In castle far away,
Guarded in ways unguessed,
Is a jewel bright as day.

Below a cliff's steep brow,
Through thickest, thorniest brake,
Past fiercest beasts must you
Your way undaunted make.

Your courage takes you in;
No door for you too stout;
The jewel bright you'll win
And, held high, bring it out.

A girl of a very finely-formed nature who was essentially sanguine needed verses which could continually counter her tendency to creep back into herself, or even to lose every vestige of courage. Through her good artistic powers she finally came out the victor.

165. Whatever all around I view
The sun a-shine makes bright

> May all I strive for, all I do
> Wear beauty's crown of light.

This was followed by the verse, "God this to the choir of the angels told" (verse 6).

166. Bifrost the Bridge unites, wondrous to see,
    Asgard and Midgard, that beauty may be.
    Down, come ye down, O divine ones, draw nigh!
    Flow through my limbs, ye powers from on high!

There followed "Heart's devotion, full and true" (verse 104).

167. In the realm of souls there is ever a singing,
    Whose sound should be heard throughout earth's lands:
    If tones creative through man's work go ringing,
    'Twill be clasped into one by beauty's fair hands.

168.   Let what would run to waste
    In form solidify:
    Through hindrance bravely faced
    Great strength I wind thereby.

The following six verses were given to a boy who was regarded in the class as a model of orderliness and devotion to duty. They were to help him to develop a counter-poise to this element in himself through religion and through art.

169. "Flower, say where is that beauty of thine!
     Down is hanging each petal and leaf."
     "Alas! I faint for new strength I pine,
     But fading, I fall towards the grave in grief."
     Came then showers and refreshing dew,
     And gentle winds cooling, quick'ning and mild.
     The flower learned thankfulness deep and true.
     To help and to thank – learn thou also, child!

170. What's safely hid in the seed's small shrine
     The spring-sun brings forth with gentle shine:
     Such a wonder unfolds into sight!
     And all that man learns and does each day
     To the stars above wings gladly its way,
     Works he ever in beauty's light.

171. How beautiful they, the moon, stars and sun!
     How glorious the earth and all thereon!
     Each herb, each beast both the great and small,
     Is wondrously graced by Him who made all.
     Even so when men their creating begin,
     May beauty divine hold sway therein!

172.   To the spirit of man gave God above
             The body for its dwelling,
             That man himself creator prove,
             His task divine fulfilling.

173.   Where tone and colour freely play,
             Man strives with utmost might

> To reconcile through beauty's sway
> The stuff of earth and heaven's light.

174.   Although this great world wide
        In strictest harmony
        Must follow God as guide,
        Machine 'twill never be.
        See thou how life at every turn shows
        The Creator as artist in all he does.

To make a verse for a child with a one-sidedness or even a downright defect in their nature is much easier than for a child with many gifts and hardly any failings. The following verses show in what direction one can try to help the latter.

175.   In life and learning love will reveal
        The secret all secrets beyond.
        "Who seeks will find" and His word fulfil
        Who above the bright stars is enthroned.

176.   He who'd rear a noble steed
        First its ways must learn to know:
        Then within it each good seed
        Tend, that these alone do grow.
        Selfless work in beauty true
        Makes the world divinely new.

177.   Wakes but the word the spirit's fire,
        Man beholds the depths of worlds.

Warms but love man's deeds, then lo!
In the light he'll ever go.

178. Every look into nature divine
Calls us upward to wisdom:
Every look into man's deep soul
Love in the heart awakens.
Powers of God weave the whole world through;
Deeds of man, may they crown creation.

The girl who received the three verses, 93, 94 and 95, that have to do with Speech and the Word was given the following two when in a younger class.

179. Seeds through the rain and the wakening sun
Sprout green after winter's chill:
Each gift of man through courage unfolds
Which creates as fire of the will.

180. The seed from which the Lord brought forth
All wonders the world contains,
From out His sounding Word had birth,
Which us and all sustains.

The last verse refers to her really marked gift for painting which was fully recognised by the rest of the class.

181. Out of warming purple and shining gold
Can life on earth its flowers unfold:

So God the Father as proof of Love
World-wisdom's circle of colours wove:
And the Angels from out their Heavens high
To the man creative with joy draw nigh.

In the education course, *The Kingdom of Childhood,* Rudolf Steiner devoted his last words to report verses, calling them "life-verses". It was a great joy to me that all the former pupils – the oldest were in their forties – to whom I spoke about the verses I had given them, still had them, treasuring them and bringing them back to me.

Bibliography

Steiner, Rudolf, *Creative Speech: the Formative Process of the Spoken Word* (CW 280) Rudolf Steiner Press, UK 1999.

–, *Faculty Meetings with Rudolf Steiner* (CW 300, 2 volumes), Anthroposophic Press, USA 1998.

–, *Foundations of Human Experience* (lectures of Aug/Sep 1919 in Stuttgart, CW 293, also published as *Study of Man)* Anthroposophic Press, USA 1996.

–, *Human Values in Education* (lectures of July 1924 in Arnhem, CW 310) Steinerbooks, USA 2005

–, *Kingdom of Childhood, The* (lectures of Aug 1924 in Torquay, CW 311) Anthroposophic Press, USA 1995

–, 'The Realm of Language,' lecture of July 17, 1915, not published in English (part of *Kunst- und Lebensfragen im Lichte der Geisteswissenschaft,* CW 162, Dornach 2000.

–, *Speech and Drama* (lectures of Sep 1924 in Dornach, CW 282) Steinerbooks, USA 2007.

–, *The Study of Man* (lectures of Aug/Sep 1919 in Stuttgart, CW 293, also published as *Foundations of Human Experience)* Rudolf Steiner Press, UK 2004.

Index